From Miracle to Miracle

Dennis Harworth

TRILOGY CHRISTIAN PUBLISHERS
TUSTIN, CA

Trilogy Christian Publishers
A Wholly Owned Subsidiary of Trinity Broadcasting Network
2442 Michelle Drive
Tustin, CA 92780

For information, address Trilogy Christian Publishing

Rights Department, 2442 Michelle Drive, Tustin, Ca 92780.

Trilogy Christian Publishing/ TBN and colophon are trademarks of Trinity Broadcasting Network.

For information about special discounts for bulk purchases, please contact Trilogy Christian Publishing.

Manufactured in the United States of America

Trilogy Disclaimer: The views and content expressed in this book are those of the author and may not necessarily reflect the views and doctrine of Trilogy Christian Publishing or the Trinity Broadcasting Network.

10 9 8 7 6 5 4 3 2 1

Library of Congress Cataloging-in-Publication Data is available.

ISBN 978-1-63769-410-7

ISBN 978-1-63769-411-4 (ebook)

Contents

Dedication

I dedicate this book to my Aunt Margaret Simpson. She has been the greatest influence and inspiration in my life to be a writer.

I also dedicate this book to my loving wife, Barbara, whose encouragement, counsel, and collaboration made the writing of this book possible.

Most importantly, I express my heartfelt gratitude to the God of miracles who graciously moves in my life. May He also show His love and give hope to each person who reads this book and give each one hope to experience His supernatural hand in their life.

Foreword

The word exuberant describes a person that is filled with or characterized by a lively energy and excitement. You can say that about someone who has a deep commitment and connection with our Lord and Savior Jesus Christ, or at least that's how it should be.

If there is a man who has met Jesus and is truly excited and grateful about the freedom of life he has received, it would be Dennis Harworth. For him, "*exuberant*" would be an understatement.

It is with great honor that I had the privilege of reading *From Miracle to Miracle*. I found myself with smiles on my face time and time again as I saw how Dennis processed the presence of God on a regular basis throughout his life. For most people, they make a commitment to God but do not do much to make sure that their commitment is fulfilled. Dennis, however, has learned how to make his commitment alive.

As you read through the book, Dennis will tell you some of the amazing happenings in his life and then give you the foundation of scripture to back up the very presence of God. It is not just a good story, but a learning time for the reader. Dennis goes beyond his commitment to the place where he sees *Jesus in everything.* Stop and think about that for a moment. Both the good and the bad of life are overshadowed by the presence of God. That is not only pleasing to God, but the solid ground for a miracle.

From Miracle to Miracle, is an expression of a mature man's deep relationship with God, and it sets goals for all of us to bring Jesus along in our lives in everything. *See Jesus in everything.* To see Jesus in everything brings with it love, joy, peace, and all the fruits of the Spirit. To live life filled with His presence and acknowledge it by seeing Jesus in each step will bring you to a place that becomes a life going from miracle to miracle.

From Miracle to Miracle is not only a good read—it is a God read.

Thank you, Dennis for being a real man of God.

Jim Cobrae, Founding Senior Pastor
Rock Church and World Outreach Center

Introduction

As we go through life, how often do we really reflect on the events and circumstances that have become our life? As I was sharing the stories of my life with my wife, she said to me one day, "Your whole life has been a miracle." It was an awakening to me that there have been many wonderful and supernatural experiences in my life. I wanted to write this book to share some of the stories with you to show that God is indeed a God of miracles and to encourage you to believe God for His best and His blessing in your life.

Miracles by definition are amazing, extraordinary events that appear to be contrary to the laws of nature and are regarded as acts of God. They are supernatural manifestations of divine power that reveal the presence and power of God. Anytime a miracle occurs, it raises interest, awe, and marvel in the eyes and minds of people. The purpose of a miracle is to display the power of God to the person who needs one and to be a witness to the unbeliever to lead them to salvation (John 20:30).

Many of the things that have happened in my life are unexplainable and have caused me to marvel at the abundant mercy and grace of God. My desire for this book is to encourage your heart and for you to come to know that with God—*nothing shall be impossible.*

Miracles themselves do not build faith. They get our attention and testify of God's mercy, grace, and love. When we witness the miracles, it draws us to God causing us to give glory to Him. The sharing of these miracles is to draw your attention to God.

Why these things have happened to me and continue to happen, I do not know. What I do know, is that our God is a God of miracles. Miracles are to point to what God is doing, to draw us closer to Him. Our Heavenly Father so loves mankind that He will work in the life of a sinner as well as a believer. The miracles are attention-getters, but it is His Word that saves, heals, restores, and brings life.

This is my story but the outcomes have nothing to do with me and everything to do with God. Let God be your source and your strength. Let Him be everything to you and watch the miracle of His love unfold in your life each and every day. I invite you to join me in this adventure as I share some snapshots of the supernatural goodness of God in my life.

CHAPTER 1

The Life That Should Not Have Been

Let's start at the beginning. When my mother was born, her mother, my grandmother, died two days after giving birth to her. This difficulty with child birth was determined to be genetic which meant that my mother also had to face this danger. Giving birth to my brother, my mother came close to death. She was advised by her doctor not to have any more children, because the next one would be fatal.

Several years passed by, but there was still such a longing in her heart for another child. There was something deep inside her that just was not satisfied. After careful consideration and much discussion with my father, my mother was determined to have another child. This was a life or death decision she was making for both her and her next child.

Four years after my brother was born, she miraculously gave birth to a healthy second son, me. That was not the end but just the beginning. I am very grateful to be able to say that my mother lived until I was 33 years old. What a blessing to have so many years with a woman as strong and courageous as my mother. There was always a special bond between us, and years later she told me that it was so worth the risk.

> *For You formed my inward parts; You covered me in my mother's womb. I will praise You, for I am fearfully and wonderfully made; marvelous are Your works that my soul knows very well*
>
> (Psalms 139:13, NKJV).

My birth should not have happened, but God had other plans and fashioned my days when as yet there were none of them.

CHAPTER 2

If Only I Could Fly

The decades of the fifties and sixties were such a different era and time in our lives. It was safe to ride your bicycle all over town, and we even drank out of the garden hose. Life was much slower and seemed to be simpler with Roy Rogers, the Lone Ranger, and Mr. Rogers having a wonderful day in the neighborhood.

This particular day, it was a cool and crisp Palm Sunday in April. At the age of eleven, I was able to enjoy riding my bicycle to and from church. The minute church was dismissed, I eagerly raced to jump on my bicycle. However, something across the street caught my attention so I decided to go and get a closer look. Not wanting to ride my bike across the street, I put down the kick stand and left it on the sidewalk.

Passing between two parked cars, I ran into the street. Much to my surprise, right next to me was the front end of a car with a shiny chrome bumper and grill. Just having come through the intersection on the green light, the driver did not have a chance to apply the brakes. I jumped as the car hit me, and I stretched out my arms straight in front of me like Superman. The road was racing by below me as I flew over the asphalt. Everything seemed to be in slow motion, and the thought came to mind that this was definitely not normal. I found myself being fascinated as I watched the road speed by below me.

Finally, with a belly flop, I landed on the ground. While in a state of shock, in one motion I leaped to my feet and leaned up against a tree with my foot propped up on the tree for support. As the couple driving the car frantically ran to see if I was okay, much to their amazement, there were no broken bones, scrapes, or cuts. There was no evidence that anything had happened except a small tear on the elbow of the red sweater I was wearing.

About that time, people were coming out of the church, and needless to say, the incident caused quite a commotion. People were bustling about trying to figure out what had happened. It was determined that I had been thrown 72 feet through the air and yet there were no signs of injury.

After much convincing that I was not hurt, the woman drove me home and her husband rode my bicycle to my house. They lived only a few blocks away and wanted to see me safely home. As we arrived at the house, the couple explained what had happened. They wanted to know right away if any signs of injury arose because they took full responsibility, even though it was not their fault. My mother just looked at me, shook her head, and said, "What am I going to do with you?" Funny thing, my wife does the same thing. I guess some things do not change.

My mother kept a close eye on me all night, and when I awoke the next morning I was perfectly fine! The only explanation for this is the protection of God. *For He shall give His angels charge over you, to keep you in all your ways. In their hands they shall bear you up, lest you dash your foot against a stone* (Psalms 91:11-12, NKJV).

This is one of the many times God, in His loving-kindness, sent His angels to keep me from harm. I really cannot explain why. It could be that He saw my future and spared my life time after time in order to fulfill His plans and purpose for me. The only thing I do know beyond a shadow of doubt is that God is faithful to His word, and His angels do their jobs well! God is able to supply supernatural protection no matter what the circumstances.

If God can bring the three Hebrews out of a fiery furnace, shut the mouth of lions for Daniel, and enabled me to walk away without a scratch from my crash landing, God can also protect you. What He did in my life and throughout the Bible, He will do for you.

God will provide protection from unimaginable danger. He will give peace and security from the fears of life and rescue us from our troubles. God Almighty even guarantees in writing satisfaction for life. You can believe Him when He promises: *I will rescue those who love me. I will protect those who trust in My name. When they call on Me, I will answer; I will be with them in trouble. I will rescue them and honor them. I will satisfy them with a long life and give them my salvation* (Psalms 91:14-16, NLT).

This blessed chapter of Psalm 91 has more promises of protection, but they are dependent upon one's meeting the conditions of the first two verses.

> *He who dwells in the secret place of the Most High shall remain stable and fixed under the shadow of the Almighty [Whose power no foe can withstand]. I will say of the Lord, He is my Refuge and my Fortress, my God: on Him I lean and rely, and in Him [confidently] trust!"*
>
> (Psalms 91:1-2, AMPC).

Can this be obtained just by loving the Lord and putting our trust in Him? Well, I don't know about you, but I need to find out exactly how to receive an offer like this. In order to meet the conditions of these amazing promises, here are two things you need to know:

Where to stay and What to say.

WHERE TO STAY

If you were to stay in protective custody at a government safe house, you would be required to follow explicit instructions for your own good. All outside contact would be totally restricted, especially to family and friends. It would be mandatory to remain indoors at all times and completely stay away from doors and windows.

In order to abide (live, stay, dwell) under the protective custody of Almighty God, you must, for your own good, follow the house rules—His house, His rules. God's house is filled with holiness (Psalm 93:5). If you want the benefits of living in His house you must live a holy life, exclusively His, set apart for Him, with simple trust and hearty obedience (1 Peter 1:15-16).

This means abstaining from all of the outside influences of the world. Be careful what you watch on television, especially the news. Guard your heart when reading newspapers and magazines with all the news of the state of the world regarding the economy, pandemics, or political races. Refuse to allow the world's views into your thinking. We want to avoid anything contrary to His ways and His will. If you abide in Him, God will not let evil dwell with you (Psalms 5:4).

As long as you remain under the shadow of His wing, you are protected. *"Because you have made the Lord, who is my refuge, even the Most High, your dwelling place,*

No evil shall befall you, nor shall any plague come near your dwelling" (Psalms 91:9-10, NKJV). When you step out from under the shadow of the Almighty, doing life your way, you are subject to the merciless onslaught of the world and demonic forces. You are vulnerable to every evil way that can come against you. God is a shelter and a refuge, a safe place. He will protect us from the evil one, from dangers and the fears of life. To do this, it is a necessity to live or dwell with Him (Psalm 91:1). In Him is where we should stay, so—STAY HOME.

WHAT TO SAY

Anytime you testify in a court of law, you swear to tell the truth, the whole truth, and nothing but the truth, so help you God. What you say as a witness can have a direct bearing on the outcome of the case. Every word spoken is recorded exactly as it was spoken, whether or not it is what you meant. Sometimes we are trapped by the words of our own mouth (Proverbs 6:2), even without some sharp and slick attorney twisting our words to their desired outcome.

Most people do not understand the power of words. God spoke words and created the heavens and the earth. Our spoken words are powerful enough to change our lives for better or worse. We must realize that death and life are in the power of the tongue (Proverbs 18:21). We can speak life into every area of our lives and have what we say (Mark 11:23). Instead, we tend to say what we have and end up being a fool (Proverbs 15:2).

Therefore, if the promises of Psalms 91 (NKJV) are to be implemented into our lives we need to obey verse two: *I will say of the Lord, He is my refuge and my fortress; My God, in Him I will trust.*

When you speak the Word of God over your life, it will sink into your heart and build your faith (Romans 10:17). When faith speaks from a heart filled with God's Word, it creates a spiritual force which brings forth the reality of God's promises. When you know what to say, you can get the promises you want. So, *SAY WHAT GOD SAYS.*

Our Heavenly Father is the Almighty God who is eternally capable of providing all the protection you need. Therefore, trust God no matter the situation or circumstances in which you live. Remember *where to stay* and *what to say* in order to live and enjoy the promises of His protection!

CHAPTER 3

Born to New Life

Growing up, I went to Catholic school for eight years and then had four years of religious classes. During that time, I was an altar boy and a choir boy and won the coveted Religion Award in the fifth grade. Surely, I thought these accolades were all that I needed to be pleasing to God. This had to mean that I was *good with God*.

Unfortunately, all this religious experience turned out to be a hindrance to receiving salvation. As life began to spiral downward in high school, I got involved with the wrong crowd and the wrong activities, such as drugs and drinking alcohol. Not to mention, just being wild and stupid.

My older brother had gotten radically saved as a young adult. He would come and share all the things that he had learned and was beginning to find out about God. Pride was in my way because of the awards and accolades, so I would not listen. After all, I already had everything I needed and was sure that I was alright with God.

My brother began to pray for me asking God how to get through the pride. I just would not listen. He was instructed by God to not back off and keep pursuing me, because my life was going downhill fast. God will give you wisdom to reach your family and friends and bring them to salvation. God's direction to him was to be wise as a serpent and gentle as a dove. In other words, don't keep pressuring—just find another way. We can miss it in life and be in a dangerous place when we think that we are *good with God* but want nothing to do with Jesus.

My brother's next approach was inviting me to a Maranatha concert hosted by Calvary Chapel on the following Saturday night. My first question was, "What's a Maranatha concert?" He said, "It is a concert where Christians get together. It is unlike anything you have ever heard before. They are rocking out with electric guitars." This began to peak my curiosity. It sounded good, but I still wasn't really interested. Then he began to lure me in, "But what is really great, while the songs are being sung, you put your arms around each other and sway to the music." He was now starting to get my attention, as I was thinking that sounds good. Then he added, "But you don't get it. You ought to see the cute girls that are there. If they are standing next to you, you can put your arms around them and sway to the music.

You might even get to meet somebody." Really!! *Now* I was interested. Forget about religion, forget about guitars, forget about the swaying to the music, I was going for the girls. The concert was approximately a one to two hour drive as it was in another city. Since we lived in Southern California, traffic patterns on the freeways can change the length of time significantly. The plan was for him to pick me up at 5:00 p.m.

The night of the concert, my parents and I went out to eat an early dinner, because I had plans with my brother to go to the concert. Conviction was already on me, so I was starting to feel the reluctance to even want to go. I decided to walk home from the restaurant and was taking my time, looking at things that I found interesting, and dawdling as much as possible. Finally, arriving home 30 minutes late, my brother was standing there waiting for me. I started making every excuse that I could because I did not want to go. You need to understand that my brother is six foot six inches tall, which is much taller than me. He doesn't get in my face very often, but with a stern voice he said, "Get in the house and change your shirt and your shoes because WE ARE GOING." Well, that got my attention, and soon we were on our way.

The entire way there, I am complaining that we would never get there on time; we won't find a parking place; we won't find a seat; why don't we just turn around blah, blah, blah! Just before we got there, my brother turned to me and said, "It is okay. God is saving two seats for us." How could he know that there are seats saved? My brother was crazy. Whatever!

As we pulled into the parking lot, it was packed. We had to park in the back corner of the lot. Now, I really want to turn around and go home, but he reassured me that God was saving two seats for us.

After walking all the way across the parking lot, we enter the very crowded foyer of the auditorium. It was literally standing room only as people were lining the walls with no place to sit. There was no way we would find seats, but my brother told me to come with him. As we walked down the aisle, twelve rows from the front there were two seats on the aisle of that row. Wow, I knew I was in trouble. God has got my number. God was saving two seats for us when it was standing room only. God did that! My brother purposely let me sit on the aisle seat.

There were three different groups performing that night. The last group was Love Song. A band which was to Christian music in the 1970s like the Beatles were to rock and roll. Love Song rocked the place with so much energy. All the songs were evangelistic, meaning they sang about Jesus and the salvation message.

When the concert was over, I was ready to go, but my brother assured me that this was the best part of the evening and we needed to stay. What did he mean the best part? Pastor Chuck Smith from Calvary Chapel Costa Mesa got up to give an altar call. Pastor Chuck, in his deep, rich, bellowing voice, started talking about the things of God. I sat there thinking, this guy doesn't know where I've been or who I am. After all, what would my friends think if I became a Christian? The moment I thought this, Pastor Chuck said, "It doesn't matter what your friends think; you are going to know Jesus." Then I thought, well what about my past, and he would answer, "It doesn't matter about your past. He wants to clean your slate and give you a future." I found myself having a conversation between my thoughts and the pastor. I would think to myself what about this and what about that, and then Pastor Chuck would immediately reply with the answer. How was this guy doing that? By this time, I was freaking out and almost to the point of getting angry because the pastor was *reading my mail*. I didn't understand what was happening and how he could do this.

He invited the audience to stand up and for those who wanted to receive Jesus to come forward to the front of the auditorium. Not me, I planted my feet, clinched my fists, and was shaking, resisting with everything that I had. Sweat was rolling down my back.

Finally, the pastor ended the invitation. Just when I thought that I was okay, he did a second altar call saying that Jesus loves you. I know He loved me because I was taught that growing up. It was then that it felt like this big hand had reached in and grabbed my heart and was pulling it out of my chest. It was tugging on my heart. Pastor Chuck said in his deep, mellow voice, "Don't you feel that tugging on your heart? That's the Lord, ask Him in." Okay, that was it, I had had enough! I looked at my brother and said that I was going forward.

As I finished saying the sinner's prayer and asking Jesus in my heart, all of my past, all the filth, all the garbage, all of the sin, all this burden was lifted off of me. I felt alive for the first time in my life. I remember looking up at the ceiling and my spirit was so light and full of life. I felt like I was doing pushups off the ceiling. What an amazing miracle; my life was transformed and my slate was cleaned.

I asked my brother later why he didn't tell me about this incredible born-again experience. Although he had tried multiple times, I had not been ready to listen. The drive home seemed so short, because I was floating all the way home, in awe of this new life. What was most wonderful, I found that the desire to do the wrong things was now gone. All desire to sin had been wiped away. Those things I had done for years now felt foreign to me.

Due to my brother's obedience to do what God had asked of him, my life has been forever changed. We may never know until we are in Heaven how even the simplest act of obedience can impact someone's life. Here is an example:

Many years later, while at church, the Lord asked me to kneel during a worship song. I was sitting in the front row and felt very conspicuous. After some coaxing from the Holy Spirit, since this was the first time I had ever done anything like this, I did as God asked. At the end of service, the Lord revealed to me that a man sitting across the sanctuary was bargaining with God asking God to show him someone who would kneel down openly to worship Him. If someone would kneel, then he would know that God is real. By my obedience to kneel, not only did he come forward during the altar call, but he brought his wife with him. God has purpose in those seemingly insignificant or unusual things. We don't know what God is doing in someone else's life. Be obedient to respond to God's leading and instruction. Someone's life may depend on it.

CHAPTER 4

Dedication and Devotion

It was my senior year in high school. These were wild and crazy days. A few months before graduation, I had accepted Jesus into my life, and it became quickly evident that although my heart had changed, my friends had not. It is impossible to try to live God's way and the world's way at the same time. It just will not work. My friends kept asking me to do the things we had always done together, but now my heart was not the same. I had changed on the inside and I did not want to do those things anymore. I kept making excuses for why I could not go with them. Excuses like I had to go to class to take a test, when previously I would ditch class at a moment's notice.

I found out the hard way that evil company corrupts good habits (1 Corinthians 15:33, NKJV). When we get saved, it is so important to start fresh with our lives. Our old friends we did evil and sinful things with will bring

us back down if we don't make changes in our friendships and associations. Mentors and godly friendships
are so important. As a young Christian, I had no one to
lead the way and point me in the direction of godliness.

I did well for a while as I continued through my senior year. But as time passed, I began to weaken and
slide away. I did not weaken in my love for God but in
my thinking and behavior. My spirit was firm, but my
flesh was pulling at me; I was torn. The carnal or sin
nature will always try to get you back into living by the
flesh.

It was Memorial Day 1972, and I went with my un-
saved friends to the beach. We all piled into my 1962
Rambler station wagon, which was a tank. Back then,
cars were made out of steel instead of the softer met-
als of today. Cars also did not come with air condition-
ing in those days. I think that is why everyone wanted
to take my car, because it was the only car among my
friends with an air conditioner.

It was a beautiful day at the beach. The sun was
warm and the waves were glassy, an especially nice day.
There were plenty of drugs and alcohol available, of
which all were partaking. We had been partying all day.
After sun, surf, and party time, we were headed home
very late at night. It was after midnight when we finally
arrived close to home. One of the girls lived in a canyon
in a remote area, and we were on our way to take her

home. The intersection going into the canyon had a two way stop sign, meaning the cross traffic did not have to stop. It was very dark, and after looking for oncoming traffic and feeling it was safe, I started across the intersection. The speed limit for the road I was crossing was 55 miles per hour, and the road went up over a small hill so it was difficult to see any distance. I could see some lights shining upward on the other side of the grade, so I began to accelerate a little to get across the intersection. As the lights came over the crest of the hill and began to flood my car, the front end of my car was just clearing the intersection. I looked to see how much time I had to get out of the way and was sure that I had cleared the path of the oncoming car. As I turned to look at the approaching car, the headlights of the approaching car were right above the window frame of the passenger door of my car. All I could do was grip the steering wheel with all the strength I could muster. This car hit us so hard that it actually bounced off and hit us a second time. My car began to spin to the right and I was holding on to that steering wheel with such force that I bent the wheel. My arms were torn off the steering wheel by the force of the impact. In desperation, I braced myself with my leg against the air conditioner to prevent me from being thrown from the car. None of us were wearing seat belts, as this was long before seat belt laws. There had been two other people in the front seat with me. There was a boy next to the door and a girl in the middle of the seat. As my arm was ripped from the steering wheel, it hit the seat and I realized that the seat was empty. They were both gone and had been ejected from the car. Just as the car stopped spinning, the driver's side door was open and my arm fell out of the door onto the pavement. As I was pulling myself up, another car that was passing by stopped immediately and asked if anyone was hurt. How fortunate that he knew first aid. It was obvious that there were multiple injuries as all but one of the passengers from my car were no longer in the car. Just as he offered his help, a sheriff was driving by, slammed on his brakes, and called for several ambulances. It was discovered later that the man who hit us had been going over 80 mph in a 55 mph zone.

We quickly surveyed the scene, and I realized that one of the guys appeared to be missing. He had been sitting in the back seat against the door. The car had hit us between the front and rear doors on the post and the rear door was completely smashed in about a foot. To our surprise, he was still in the car but was enveloped by the car door. The door came in right up to his chest and the metal literally bent right around him. It looked like the door was going right through him but actually just wrapped around him. My heart sank, as I thought he was dead. The police officer and I, with fearful hesitation, walked over to him. As we got near, we heard him moan as he began to come to. Miraculously, he was okay. We had to pry him out sideways and finally freed him from the car with only minor injuries. We continued to search for the other passengers and as all of my friends were found, we were loaded into ambulances and transported to the hospital.

The fact that a man who knew first aid was there to help, that the sheriff arrived immediately, and the ambulances were there within ten minutes was miraculous. Just two days later, in that exact same place, a teenage girl was killed in another accident. The same ambulance company took 45 minutes to arrive at the scene. The witnesses had time to go to the girl's home and get her father who was a doctor and return to the accident scene before the ambulance arrived. Here he was, working on his daughter, trying to save her life, before the ambulance finally arrived. She ended up losing her life. This incident was instrumental in getting the speed limit changed, a signal installed, and the slope of the hill flattened. Her life was a big price to pay for these needed changes!

We were at the hospital in the emergency room. Since my injuries were minimal, I was in the hallway on a stretcher. The three with more serious injuries were being worked on in various rooms. The young man who was in the back seat only needed three stitches and was released to go home. That was miraculous in itself.

As I was waiting on the stretcher, in a state of bewilderment, I did not know what to do. The fact that people were hurt, I was struggling to come to grips with. When the doctor came out of the rooms where he had been attending to the two boys, he looked at me and his eyes dropped to the floor. He said that there was nothing more that could be done. Their blood pressure was dropping and their vitals were weak. The doctors had done all that they could do. When I asked about the condition of the girl, I was informed that she was paralyzed from the waist down. She should make it, but she would be paralyzed.

Deep despair set in as the reality of the day was crashing in on me. It is so important to remember that God is a very present help in time of need. I began to seek God and ask Him, "What am I going to do?" Then, God reminded me that just three months earlier I had received Him into my life at a Maranatha concert. With my deepest heart-felt prayer, I went before the Lord and said, "If You will save their lives like You saved mine, I will commit my life to You for the rest of my life." Within 30 minutes, the vital signs stabilized and the blood pressure began to rise to normal on the two boys who were so critical. They regained consciousness, and the paralysis *mysteriously* left the girl. The doctors could not explain it. All of us had lived through the night and were eventually able to go home. As I visited my friend with the three stitches, I was able to lead him in the sinner's prayer to receive Jesus. The girl eventually got saved and later wrote a book.

After the accident and fully committing my life to Jesus, I still needed instruction in the ways of God. There was a man where I worked that would sit down at lunch time and open up the Bible. One day, we ran into each other as we were leaving work, and I decided to ask him a question, but a completely different question came out of my mouth: "How do you grow in your walk with the Lord," I asked? He knew that our encounter was not by accident but a God-ordained meeting. He looked at me and said, "That wasn't what you originally wanted to say, was it?" The Holy Spirit knows how to get our attention and to draw us to Him.

How could he know that? He told me as he was praying and reading the Bible that morning, he was told that God was going to open a door for someone. The Holy Spirit will tell you of things to come (John 16:13). His instruction to me was to get into a church fellowship that teaches the Word of God. Fellowship with other believers is so vital to our spiritual walk, growth, and maturity. Spending time reading His Word and communing with Him through prayer is essential to growing in God's ways.

I must admit, however, this commitment over the years has not always been easy. I had to learn to stick with this walk of faith, especially when there weren't any *feel-good* feelings. We must realize faith does not depend on feelings, and you cannot take a break from your commitment. It is actually a continuous process with many ups and downs to deal with in order to stay the course. Being truly committed helps you trust God completely while He gets you through the trials and tribulations. Being devoted to the things of God keeps you focused on His plans for your life. This also gives you the ability to achieve goals that you might have only dreamed about.

The Bible magnificently describes God's faithfulness to His Word. These verses thoroughly sum up my life: *Trust in the Lord and do good, dwell in the land and feed on His faithfulness. Delight yourself also in the Lord, and He shall give you the desires of your heart. Commit your way to the Lord, trust also in Him and He shall bring it to pass* (Psalms 37:3-5, NKJV).

They have become my all-time favorite verses of scripture, particularly when I get off track in life and need God's specific direction and promises from His Word. This is especially true of verse five. Since that night many years ago in the hospital, I have learned what it means to commit myself to the Lord. It means entrusting everything—all that we are and all that we have —to His sovereign Lordship. *For if Jesus is not Lord of all, He is not Lord at all.*

To commit our lives to the Lord is to trust Him (Psalms 37:5) to lead us, guide us, guard us, and to direct us in the way and manner in which we are to go. It was a great revelation when I realized that God is smarter than me, and He knows what is best for me. He will bring to pass what I have committed and entrusted to Him in the best possible way—for me!

God will always be faithful to His Word. It is up to us to learn about the conditions of commitment to get God's guaranteed promises. Here are three ways to deepen your understanding of commitment:

COMMIT YOUR WAY – Trust God in where you are going!

Psalm 37:5 says it very plainly, *"Commit your way to the Lord, trust also in Him, and He shall bring it to pass."* To *commit* literally means to roll, to roll down, to roll away, and to remove. It is a picture of a camel unloading a heavy load by kneeling down and leaning far to one side to roll off the entire burden. Once the load is in motion, it is committed, and there is no stopping it. The *way* is your journey down the path or road of life. So to *commit your way* to the Lord means to roll the actions and behavior of your way of doing life upon the Lord, while entrusting everything to Him.

Many times in high school I was told that I was heading down the wrong path. I sure did not see it that way, because I thought I was right to do my own thing.

There is a way that seems right to a man, but its end is the way of death (Proverbs 14:12, NKJV). By God's grace, I turned and trusted Him before I came to the end of the road. Since that day, I have walked this amazing journey with Jesus with no regrets and no looking back. As long as I *stay the course* of trusting God, my life continues to be *beyond my highest prayers, desires, thoughts, hopes and dreams* (Ephesians 3:20, AMPC).

It is my desire that you too may enjoy such a sweet promise from God. He shall bring to pass whatever has been committed and entrusted to Him. It won't be easy, but it will come to pass in a far greater way than you can imagine. You may not know exactly where your life with Jesus will take you, but that is why you need to trust God in where you are going.

So, *COMMIT YOUR WAY!*

Living by faith is walking out God's plan for you when circumstances contradict what you are believing God for.

COMMIT YOUR WORKS – Trust God in what you are doing!

Commit your works to the Lord, and your thoughts will be established (Proverbs 16:3, NKJV). I like what this verse says, but I thoroughly enjoy how the Amplified Bible Classic edition states this verse: *Roll your works upon the Lord [commit and trust wholly to Him; He will cause your thoughts to become agreeable to His will, and] so shall your plans be established and succeed.* Once again, commit and trust are paired up to show the importance of what God is saying and what He will do. Your works are your actions or activity. In the Hebrew, this word is a combination of *what!* (an excited expression) and *do* or *make* with the connotation of ethical obligation or obedience (Hebrew Lexicon). In other words, God will bless what you are doing when you trust His Word and act according to what the Word says.

On the other side, God will not bless your mess when it is *doing your own thing your way.* But wait! The best part of the promise is yet to come. After you have committed your works, *He will cause your thoughts to become agreeable to His will and so shall your plans be established and succeed.* Read this again slowly, and let it really sink in. If you commit and trust all your actions *to God,* He will cause *your plans* to prosper and succeed. This is not a casual level of commitment but an all-in commitment. When you trust and depend completely on God, He will empower *you* to do the works you have committed to Him.

I can tell you firsthand that doing things God's way brings His wonderful, amazing, and marvelous results! Trusting God might involve an element of risk, but it always yields the richest rewards. That is why it is essential to trust God in what you are doing.

So, *COMMIT YOUR WORKS!*

Your level of success and prosperity is directly related to the level of your commitment.

COMMIT YOUR WILL – Trust God in what you are deciding!

The first verse of Romans chapter 12 in the Amplified Bible Classic edition, Paul the Apostle appeals and begs you to make a decisive dedication of your body—presenting all your members and faculties—as a living sacrifice, holy (committed, consecrated), and well pleasing to God, which is your reasonable (rational, intelligent) service and spiritual worship. Verse two goes on to say, *And do not be conformed to this world, but be transformed by the renewing of your mind, that you may prove what is that good and acceptable and perfect will of God.* In a nutshell, your committed sacrifice to God should be the sensible thing to do. For while renewing your mind, you will find out God's perfect will for you.

One of the best things you could do is to know the good, and acceptable, and perfect will of God. For once you are transformed in your mind, it becomes so much easier to make right choices. This is because your will is the part of the mind that makes decisions. Therefore, when you commit your will to God, you will enjoy knowing what is good for you. And at the same time, it will please God. This is why you need to trust God in what you are deciding.

So, *COMMIT YOUR WILL!*

God's plans are your destiny. Your plans are your reality. When your plans line up with God's plans that is when your destiny becomes your reality.

God always wants what is best for you and is faithful to keep each and every promise in His Word. He will not force them into your life, but He does guarantee to bring them to pass if you will commit and trust your life to a loving God. I had to find out the hard way in a life and death situation with the car accident. Please don't wait until then. God will reward your dedication and devotion to Him by empowering you to enjoy His purpose in your life in *where you are going,* prosperity in your plans in *what you are doing,* and pleasure in His will in what you are deciding.

So, COMMIT YOUR WAY, YOUR WORKS, AND YOUR WILL TO HIM!

CHAPTER 5

Don't Give Up

It was a sparkling spring day as a co-worker and I went to play some one-on-one basketball. The first person to reach 21 points was the winner, with each basket being one point. Although I thoroughly enjoyed playing basketball, I was a little reluctant to play against someone who was so much taller, stronger, and could jump a lot higher than me. Suspecting that I was outmatched, I decided to go for it anyway.

My suspicions were soon confirmed as he totally dominated the game. He was hitting shots from everywhere. He was unstoppable, close to the basket, and easily got the rebounds of my missed shots. His intense defense completely frustrated me and made it extremely difficult to even dribble, much less to score. With the score now, 18-3 in his favor, utter discouragement had set in, and I was losing hope of ever winning the game.

Then a clear, commanding, yet loving voice loudly told me, "Don't give up!" The voice was so loud that I thought for sure it was audible. I thought the Lord was standing right beside me telling me, "Don't give up!" But when no one else heard anything, I quickly became very attentive to make sure I was actually hearing from God. The Lord *immediately* reminded me, "You can do all things through MY anointing. I will strengthen you" (Philippians 4:13). This touched the very core of my being and energized me to a new level. All of a sudden, I could see myself being able to do what I had not been able to do the whole game. Not only was I able to score, but I stopped him from scoring. All he needed to do was score just three more points and he would win the game. The more I saw myself winning and the more I scored, the more my energy picked up and my confidence soared. Because God had told me, "Don't give up," I became extremely expectant and convinced of what I was able to do. To the absolute amazement of my opponent, I made an incredible comeback and won the game.

Have you ever felt hopeless, being so far behind in something that you were ready to give up? Are you on the brink of despair with nowhere to turn for some answers? Well, according to the Word of God, you do not have to stay there. The Lord plans to give you a future and a hope (Jeremiah 29:11). He has given you exceeding great and precious promises (2 Peter 1:4), and you can be fully persuaded that what He has promised, He is able also to perform (Romans 4:21). Get to know what

God promises. If you don't know what they are, you are without hope. However, if you know and act on His promises, you will live in earnest expectation and hope, being ashamed of nothing. This is a double assurance from God. Hope is intense anticipation and expectation with confidence in what God promises!

So just know, it doesn't matter how small the problem or how big the situation, God wants to give you hope. You can be in earnest expectation of being healthy and whole. You can intensely expect success and prosperity in your life, your marriage, and your children. You can be in eager anticipation of achieving God's best in your business, your education, or whatever pertains to your life. Why? Because what you are earnestly expecting is not dependent on medicine, the economy, your spouse, or other people. It is based on the covenant promises of Almighty God. Because He said it, you can be filled with hope and earnestly expect it!

Life is more than a basketball game, but what a lesson I learned from acting on His Word. Yes, I had to put forth the effort, but I didn't give up hope. The more the hope grew, the better the situation got, and the more confident I became. The greatest blessing was not in learning the lesson or winning the game, but this act of obedience of not giving up eventually led to the other player becoming a Christian.

Therefore, if things are at the worst they can possibly be, or even a seemingly minor situation, it doesn't matter to God—don't give up! Listen to Him and obey His Word. You can literally do all things through Christ which strengthens you (Philippians 4:13), just don't give up! When facing impossible challenges, hear the Lord say, *"Fear not, for I am with you; be not dismayed, for I am your God. I will strengthen you, Yes, I will help you, I will uphold you with My righteous right hand"* (Isaiah 41:10, NKJV). Stand on God's Word and His precious and personal promises to you, then watch hope rise up within you. You can have the intense anticipation and expectation with confidence in all that God promises if you—

DON'T GIVE UP!

CHAPTER 6

Alone But Not Forsaken

It is so important to live life God's way. I had been a Christian for 25 years and thought that I was living life according to God's Word. However, when my life came crashing down around me, it was apparent that something was not as it should be. Like the nation of Israel, so many times they saw the greatness of God yet turned to live life their own way. Let me explain.

Because I was doing life in my own strength and not trusting God, I got this *brilliant* idea to provide for my family by adding and doing more and more jobs. At one point, I had five jobs and was working as much as 100 hours per week. There was very little time left for family and a quality life. As a result, my marriage ended in a bitter divorce, which alienated me from my daughters. And to top it off, I lost my jobs in which I had put my trust. There was no place to live and no money coming in. Devastated over losing everything and now all alone, there was a very looming question: Now what? When you hit the bottom in life, it causes much soul searching and the asking of many more questions.

Fortunately, my brother helped me to move into a house that he had previously managed more than a year before and still had the keys. The house had been abandoned and forsaken by the owner who lived in another state. It was severely neglected and in a very rough neighborhood. The weeds in the yard were waist high and the windows were broken.There was no gas for heat and no running water and the roof leaked profusely, causing the wood parquet floor to be black, moldy mush. To add insult to injury, because this was a corner lot, the neighbors used the front yard as a drive by trash can.

So with deplorable conditions, no income, no utilities, no furniture, and seemingly no way out, deep depression set in. With no focus and direction for my life, I would stay curled up on the floor for days. Even the cockroaches would crawl under me to try to stay warm from the winter cold.

I came to the realization that one of two choices had to be made: stay depressed and give up *or* find a way to move forward. It was obvious that nothing was getting better on its own, so I mustered up all the inner strength I could and decided that I cannot keep living like this.

It was then I *happened* to remember reading where God says, *He is a very present help in time of trouble* (Psalm 46:1, NKJV). I knew I really needed help *now*! I also knew that I had a big part to play in all of this. I could not continue to lie on the floor doing nothing and expect life to get suddenly better.

Since finding work and getting some money coming in was very important, I created a job out of finding a job. After 72 applications and much perseverance, a union job *finally* opened up to be an auto transporter. It was a wonder that I survived my first few years at this job. If it had not been so challenging to get a job, I would have quit the first week as this was a very difficult and dangerous job.

The work available when I first started working for this company was sporadic and I would work maybe one or two days a week and usually the night shift. The most unpredictable scenario was when I was put *on call*. This means that there is no scheduled work in the foreseeable future. It also meant that I had to be ready to respond and report to work at any time. This made it difficult to plan anything because I did not know if and when I would be called to work. There were times that the on call status became a temporary layoff which could be up to a couple of months of no work. My circumstances were still very difficult, and I still could not see how this was going to change. God was about to show me His ways and how to turn my situation back into a life worth living.

It was still the first year of my employment and I was laid off the week of Christmas. I was told that it might be middle to late February before work was available. Fortunately, to my surprise, I was called back to work the last three days in January. Don't you know that God will present us with choices along the way?

As it turned out, that week was a special seminar at the church I was attending. The speaker was presenting a *Financial Freedom* seminar. I really wanted to attend, but I knew that I needed to work. I was determined to hear what the speaker had to say and since I was not able to attend the seminar, I purchased the tapes instead. You remember cassette tapes. What a great thing to have the tapes because I listened to them over and over.

It was the turning point in my life. It felt like the message was speaking right to me. It showed me how important it is to put God first in my finances through tithing, generosity, and sowing and reaping. All this time of being a Christian for more than 25 years, I came to realize that I was not a tither. I gave money, but I did not tithe. Right in the midst of my circumstances of living in this broken down house, hardly working, barely surviving and staying alive, I needed this wakeup call.

The Bible says that you are cursed with a curse because you have robbed God of tithes and offerings (Malachi 3:8). It was no wonder my life was such a mess. I had been robbing God for years. To make matters worse, I was foolishly mad at God for my circumstances, even though they were due to my choices, not God's.

When I heard this was the only place in the Bible where God tells us to test Him, I took Him up on it. It is a good thing that God is longsuffering and merciful, because I yelled at the ceiling in anger at God, "YOU said to put YOU to the test to bring all the tithes into the storehouse. Well I am going to do just that, and I AM GOING TO TEST YOU! I will play by your rules and find out exactly what YOU said in the Bible and follow it to a T. If YOU don't come through, then we are through!"

I am happy to report to you that God definitely came through. After only two months, for the first time in 17 years, I was able to cover my living expenses and pay the minimum payment on all 19 credit card debts and loans on time. Late payments and bounced check charges can get very costly. To this day, I cannot explain how this was done. It was mathematically impossible. All I can say is BUT GOD! At this point, the revelation of God's command to tithe began to sink deep into my heart. I decided right then and there that tithing would be a priority in my life—no matter how low the income and/or how high the bills. The understanding came that it does not matter how long it will take to get out of debt, I am going to be faithful to what God says. God will take care of the rest. I just need to trust Him.

Do not think for a minute that it was always easy. The temptation was there to question my ability to tithe. My income was small and my debts were large. This is where faith and trust in God's Word has to become a reality. Once tithing became a part of my life, God backed His Word, opened up the windows of heaven, and began blessing me. My whole life began to blossom and flourish. Doing life God's way is the right path to blessing and goodness. It all started with the Word of God. I spoke His word, I did according to His word, and I got God's results.

When I first began to tithe, my income was 160 dollars per week before taxes. My total debt was nearly 50,000 dollars. It did not take much calculating to know that this was an impossible scenario. God began to give me wisdom on stewardship and how to manage my finances. I established a budget and a debt reduction plan. When you manage the resources that God entrusts to you, no matter how little or much, He will bless it and cause it to multiply.

Little by little, I started to get the house and yard cleaned up and began to improve my surroundings and situation. More hours became available at work and income began to increase. I was able to pay all my bills and my debts began to decrease. To this day, I still don't know how it was possible except to say that with God all things are possible! My life was getting set in order. With God's blessing at work, in my life, and with much supernatural involvement, in two years and two months I was debt free. There are so many ways that God was present in my finances, from supernatural debt reduction to increasing my income through wisdom, and blessing the company where I worked. It is so important to not limit God in your thinking or your trust. God is an infinite God, who has great ability to turn your life around and fill it with His goodness.

The house was parallel to my life; when I moved in, it was broken and in need of much help. Now, as a faithful tither, my life and this house began to transform and become something to behold. God's transforming power had turned my life around.

One example of the miracles of God's provision was when the bathroom was being upgraded. There was only 20 dollars available to spend on new flooring. Back then, linoleum was very popular and I wanted a particular type of linoleum. While I was praying, God gave me the name of a flooring place in the neighboring county. He told me that in their warehouse, which was a separate building from the retail store, on the third row back and on the fourth shelf up was the remnant of linoleum exactly the size that I needed and the style that I wanted.

When I arrived and told the clerk what I needed, he said they did not have such a thing. I told him where to go to look for it and he looked at me like I was crazy. I asked him to please go look, and if it was there, then I would buy it. He walked away muttering to himself, but when he returned he had a look of astonishment on his face. He asked me, "How did you know?" I told him that I prayed and asked God for what I wanted and what I could afford. God gave me a picture of this store with the name on the front and where in the warehouse it was located. The clerk said that he found that hard to believe, but then he sold it to me for 20 dollars.

No matter how extreme your circumstances are, God is so much greater and will honor His Word. Do life God's way according to His Word. It is so worth it. After three years, my life and this run down, abandoned house were transformed. I was ready to move on and moved out of this house. Because of God's blessing and doing things God's way, this house was now the best looking home in the neighborhood. It was no longer broken down. And like this house, my life was now thriving. God is a restorer and can turn your life around. God turns our mourning into dancing. I had lost everything, but now I was getting married to the love of my life, which is a story for another chapter.

CHAPTER 7

The Power to Overcome

There was an incident when I had to push start a fully loaded semi-truck. The story actually begins a few months before. I was working a part-time job for an inventions submission company which had a company-wide meeting in Mazatlán Mexico that year. We were flown first class to Mexico and stayed at the Marriot Hotel situated directly on the beach.

This trip was a turning point in my life. I could leave behind the man people expected or knew from my past. I could be the man that I wanted to be and all that I desired to be for God. I wanted to be complete: spirit, soul, and body.

Early in the morning, my first priority was to spend time in God's Word. After that, with a wonderful gymnasium in the hotel, I would get a great workout before attending the company meetings. As a perk of the trip, in the free time there were excursions that the company paid for each attendee to enjoy.

One morning in my Bible study time, the Holy Spirit really impressed upon me the power of God. Not only how the power of God works, but that it will work in us and through us if we use what God has given us. This was so exciting to me, I woke up my roommate, being a believer also, and just had to share with him this wonderful revelation. God gives us supernaturally the power to live life, to walk in His ways, to share our faith, and the power to submit our will to His. God also gives us power in our physical bodies.

In the story of Samson, the Spirit of God came upon Samson and he did great feats. We don't know if his stature was muscular or just an ordinary man, but when the Spirit of the Lord came upon him, he did amazing exploits of supernatural strength.

After the meetings for the day, Wayne, my roommate and I, chose an excursion which was a tour of the city. He had a translating device, which compared to today's technology was pretty primitive. That afternoon, with device in hand, we felt secure and figured we would get along just fine. We boarded a bus which was about one-third the size of a regular school bus able to seat 15 to 20 people. As we toured the city, the driver and others on the bus were talking in Spanish. As the afternoon progressed, we turned onto a road that started out paved but soon became a dirt road. All of a sudden, we realized that we were in the jungle. On the translator device, we were trying to figure out how to say, "Where are we going?" The driver just kept driving further and further up into the hills. The daylight was beginning to turn to dusk and we knew that the further up this hill we went the longer it would take to get back to the city and our hotel. There were no street lights because it was the jungle and it is starting to get dark. The road continued to wind through the trees and finally we reached a small plateau area with a few small huts. It was like a tourist trap. They knew the passengers would be tired and hungry so they offered refreshments, which we could purchase, of course. There was nothing to eat or drink for miles except these modest refreshments. It was going to be about a ten minute break from the bus ride so we purchased a few items to refresh ourselves.

The bus driver returned to start the bus so we could begin the journey back. However, the bus would not start! Two men from inside a hut and two others along with Wayne decided to push the bus to get it going. They are all pushing with all they had at the back of the bus, but it is only moving slightly and not enough to start the bus. As I was sitting on a bench watching this take place, God brought to my remembrance the study from that morning about the power of God—His dunamis power. I jumped to my feet and said to Wayne, "Remember this morning?" As I flexed my arms and did a flex stance to show strength, I yelled, "Dunamis, the power of God. We can use the power of God." Because I was now shouting and running toward the bus, it so shocked the men that were pushing the bus that they stepped back. They surely thought that I was some crazy guy. I ran to the back of the bus and just starting pushing and kept pushing until it started moving. With enough forward motion, the driver popped the clutch and it started right up. We quickly piled back on the bus, laughing and excited that we were finally on our way back to the hotel.

Fast forward four months later, I was working for an auto transport company as a driver and I had been laid off since the week before Christmas. It made it very difficult to enjoy Christmas not knowing if I would get to return to work. At that time, I was a member of a large union which provided medical benefits if you worked a minimum of 40 hours during the month.

To complicate matters, a family member covered on the plan was diagnosed with possible breast cancer. The pressure was on to maintain the benefits, because if the coverage lapsed then this diagnosis would have been considered a pre-existing condition.

Finally, on the last three days of January 1997, I was able to go back to work. I had three days in which to work 40 hours. This was not usually a problem because a typical work day could be 12 to 15 hours. During the first two days I had worked 29 hours and had only 11 hours left for the final day. Working the night shift, the load was difficult and it took until eleven o'clock at night to get it ready for transport. I only needed five more hours to complete the minimum requirement for the health benefits. I got inside the truck and turned the ignition key, and the only sound I heard was *click, click, click*. I tried again, but the same *click, click, click*. It would not start. I was alone in the truck yard except for the night supervisor, and I asked if he could give me a jump start. Because he was not a union member, he was not authorized to do that task. A mechanic must be called. However, since it was at night, the mechanics had all gone home. The night supervisor said I would have to clock out and go home and leave the load for another day. This was the last day of the month. Leaving was not an option as I needed the hours to get the medical benefits.

Wondering how I would get the truck started, I asked God what to do, and He said, "Remember the bus. I will give you the strength." Yes, I had pushed a small bus that was empty, but this was a fully loaded truck weighing about 80,000 pounds. God said, "Remember what My Word says, the Spirit of the Lord came upon him and Samson did great feats." I said a questioning,

"Okay?" I then released the air pressure on the brakes, put it in neutral, and started pushing. The night supervisor thought I was crazy (this seems to be a common thread) and absolutely nuts trying to tell me that it was impossible to push the truck myself. I responded that by the power of God, I was going to push start this truck. Turning a deaf ear, I refused to listen to him and continued pushing on the truck. As I pushed with all my might, it was hardly budging. All of a sudden, I felt the Spirit of God come upon me. Wow, the truck began moving. One step, two steps, three steps, the truck was moving. I jumped in the truck and *vroom* the engine started. Wow, what a relief, because I was able to make my deliveries and finished the needed 40 hours. What was even better, my family member did not have cancer after all.

The next time I was in my employer's office, others were asking me how I got the truck started. They were asking the night supervisor, and he refused to tell them because he said they would not believe him even if he told them. He was the only witness and would not tell how it happened.

Even though he would not say anything, I said that I would tell them what happened. I told them that I had to push start the truck. They all thought that I was joking. No joke, the power of God came upon me and I literally push started an 80,000 pound truck. That is 40 tons. Of course, they didn't believe me, but I had no other way to explain it. The night supervisor was in such shock at what he witnessed, and he would not confirm my story.

This event started with the Word and the revelation of the power of God that is available to us in every area of our life. Being able to put God's Word to use that day to push start the truck was like David when he killed Goliath. He remembered the bear and the lion, so a giant was no big deal. The Word is the same, whether it is a small bus or a fully loaded truck, because all things are possible with God. I started that truck, and that was the miracle that really helped my life in faith.

Know what God's Word says, follow the Word, listen to the Word, speak the Word, do the Word, and you will get God's results. In the natural, our bodies stop growing taller. Unfortunately, they seem to still grow wider. We cannot change our height nor do anything about it. Our spirit, however, must continue to grow, and we are responsible for the process of the growth.

How we participate in the process of spiritual growth starts with obeying the Word. Throughout the Word, there are many reassurances from God Himself and the biggest condition to His promises is the small yet powerful word *IF. IF you diligently observe to do.* (Exodus 15:26, NKJV). *Now it shall come to pass, IF you diligently obey the voice of the Lord your God, to observe carefully all His commandments which I command you today, that the*

Lord your God will set you high above all nations of the earth. And all these blessings shall come upon you and overtake you, because you obey the voice of the Lord your God (Deuteronomy 28:1-2, NKJV). Notice it says that *if* you obey *then* the blessings will come upon you and overtake you.

It comes down to this that in order to obey the Word, you have to believe the Word. You must believe what God says is true. If you don't believe what He says, then it won't carry any weight or value. If the Word does not have any weight or value to you then you will not respect what God says. *I will have respect unto thy statutes continually* (Psalm 119:17, KJV). In order to obey God, you have to believe Him.

In its simpler Old Testament meaning, obedience signifies to hear, to listen, and to keep. It carries with it the ethical significance of hearing with reverence and obedient agreement. In the New Testament, a differ-ent origin is suggestive of hearing under or of submitting one's self to the command of authority by person or thing heard, hence to obey.

Christ Himself is the greatest illustration of obedience. *He humbled Himself, becoming obedient even unto death, yea, the death of the cross* (Philippians 2:8, KJV). Our obedience to Jesus is a supreme test of faith in Him, because by obedience to Him we are made partakers of His salvation.

Of course, knowing these things and doing these things can be very challenging. Because we live in a fallen world, there will be obstacles to our obedience to God's Word. Our old nature is sinful and carnal. It will do evil even when we want to do what is right. When we walk in the flesh or sin nature it is opposite from what the Holy Spirit wants for us, which is to walk in the Spirit. The Spirit give us desires that are opposite from what the sinful nature desires. These two forces, the flesh and the spirit, are constantly fighting each other, and our choices are never free from this conflict. If your sinful nature controls your mind, there is turmoil and death. If the Holy Spirit controls your mind, there is peace and life.

Refusing to hear from God is the first step
of willful disobedience.

Another obstacle to obedience is ignorance. Some people think that if they do not know what the Word says, then they do not have to obey it. There is a saying in the world that ignorance is bliss, which could not be further from the truth. Ignorance of God's Word can lead to death not life. God's Word is not there for us to pick and choose what verses we like or do not like. It is there for us to obey. We are not to try to bend the Word of God to fit our lifestyle, but we are to let the Word of

God transform us into His image and likeness. This is why it is so important to study the Word, listen to what God says, and just do it! It is much easier to do what God tells us to do than to deal with the consequences of not doing it.

There are countless benefits to obeying the Word of God. It is up to us to do our part. We can trust our loving Heavenly Father and realize that He will not ask of us anything that He will not empower us to complete. I want to encourage you to take this to heart and you will have the awesome privilege of watching the Lord accomplish great things in you and through you.

CHAPTER 8

Backward Plunge

The first year that I was working for the auto transport company, I was the bottom driver in seniority, which meant I got the worse loads and the oldest equipment. It was a time in my life where I was trying to get my feet back on more solid ground financially. At this point, I was just trying to catch up and pay my bills. So, consequently, I could not afford rain gear.

It was a dark, stormy wintery night. It was raining very hard, and the rain quickly covered the asphalt parking lot. I was working the night shift and I was using an unfamiliar truck. There are many components to the trucks and not being familiar with a particular truck can be hazardous. The top deck railing of the trailer where the vehicles are loaded is about ten feet above the ground. After loading a car onto the top deck of this truck, I had to exit the vehicle onto the railing which is only two and a half inches wide.

Up until that time, all cars had door handles with push buttons that had to be pushed in order to open the door. The new cars were just beginning to introduce pull handles that opened the car door when you simply pull on the handle. This particular car had one of these new handles. When I got out of the car and shut the door, I began to carefully slide my feet across the railing to get to the closest ladder on the front edge of the truck in order to climb down. Since this was not my truck, I was not familiar with the condition of the vehicle. What I did not know was that a couple feet away from where I had exited the car, there was a metal plate that had been welded on the rail to fix a crack in the metal frame of the super structure. The steel plate stuck up about a half inch above the railing. Carefully sliding my feet along, in the rain, I did not see the plate. My foot caught the edge of the plate and it caused me to lose my balance.

I felt myself beginning to fall backwards, and I desperately grabbed for the car. Because of the rain, the car was wet and slippery. I was pawing at the car trying to hold on, trying to get closer to the car to avoid falling. Instinctively, I reached for the car handle, to pull myself up. Much to my surprise, the car door opened. As a result, I fell straight back to the ground ten feet below, but something amazing happened. I did not hit the ground. It was like someone caught me and gently laid me on the ground. I was now lying on the ground in a stupor as shock began setting in. I tried to gather my thoughts and wondered what just happened.

Looking up, I saw the car door was still open ten feet above me. As the water from the wet asphalt began to soak through my clothing, I came to an awareness of what really happened. I had just fallen backwards over ten feet. Very carefully, I began to move my hands and shoulders, then my feet. Is anything broken? Do I feel any pain? There was nothing! I stood up, realizing that I did not feel the contact with the ground. Sitting down in another car to compose myself, I pondered once again what had just happened. Gratitude began to flood over me as I realized that God's hand of protection was upon me. I was miraculously saved from harm as someone caught me and gently laid me on the ground.

God has so many promises in His Word to those who believe. Psalms 91:11-12 in the New Living Translation promises, *"For He will order His angels to protect you wherever you go. They will hold you up with their hands so you won't even hurt your foot on a stone."* Praise God that His thoughts are not our thoughts, nor His ways our ways. I had experienced an unexpected miracle. God is faithful to His word and He is always ready and willing to do these amazing, mighty works in your life. God is so present in our lives in so many ways. It will not be until we are in Heaven, face to face with Jesus, that we will realize all the ways God has expressed Himself to us through His goodness, protection, blessing, and provision. Yes, I have experienced life and death situations where God has intervened. Yet, it is in the small, intimate things God does that you can really experience His love and goodness.

One day, walking in a park near our home, my wife and I stopped at an overlook point to enjoy the view of the valley and the city below us. The story of how I met my wife is in the next chapter. While we were standing there, a monarch butterfly landed on a flower just a few feet away. It spread its wings to soak in the afternoon sun. Usually, a butterfly is flittering and flying around, but this one did not move. We began to look closely at the beauty and intricate patterns on its wings. We noticed how delicate the wing structure was and the colorful array of yellow and orange carefully arranged. Looking closer to see the white dots lining the wings and the black outlines and how they intricately weave their way across each wing. The butterfly just sat there for the longest time, and we watched silently, enjoying this wonderful sight, all the while marveling at God's creation. From the fierceness of a lion and the size and strength of an elephant, to the delicate beauty of a butterfly, God has truly given us all things richly to enjoy.

Do not miss these intimate God moments when He gives you a special gift. It is so easy to be busy with life and not see the very thing that God wants to impart or just simply share with you. Take time to literally stop and smell the roses. You may discover a special blessing in the beauty of His creation.

CHAPTER 9

Cruise of a Lifetime

In my single years, after my first marriage came to an end, I was part of the singles ministry at church. I was so grateful to have a place to fellowship and meet other Christian singles. During the summer, different people from the group planned barbecues or game nights at their houses. One of the barbecues was put on by a woman named Barbara. She had handed out flyers with her address and the information for the barbecue. Unfortunately, I was not able to go that night but I kept the flyer.

It was a small gathering of five people and they decided to do something for fun. It was decided to plan a cruise and see who would want to go. The cruise was planned for January of the coming year. When the sign-ups were closed, there were four women and four men who signed up to go. I wanted to go but had no money and did not have any time available to take off work. As it turned out, the eight that had signed up were either couples or wanted to be a couple with someone going.

Since the trip was booked in July for the following January, many things can change along the way. One of the men that had signed up to go had met another woman and no longer wanted to go on the cruise. This opened up one paid spot for a man. Normally, the cruise lines will not let you transfer a paid trip to another person, but they said that it could be done. I immediately said I would go but now had to get off work. It was a seven day cruise to the Mexican Riviera, stopping at Cabo San Lucas, Mazatlán, and Puerto Vallarta, and it was a fully paid trip.

When I asked my employer for the unpaid time off, it just so happened (there are no coincidences with God) that my boss was saving up to go on a cruise and he knew the value of what was being offered to me. I was given permission to go and began looking forward to getting away and just having some fun. It was seven days to just kick back and enjoy myself. I was not going for any reason but to have a great time.

The day arrived and all eight of us piled into two cars to carpool. When we arrived at the ship and got checked in through a lengthy process, the transfer fee that I thought I would have to pay was waived. The four women bunked together and the four men bunked together. It was interesting to be crammed into very small staterooms with 4 bunks in each room. That was an adventure in itself. It was very close quarters with people you don't really know and one bathroom for each group, especially one bathroom for four women. Wow. Obviously, by the end of the week we got to know each other much better.

For each meal we were seated at the same table for eight. The meals we shared were some of the most enjoyable times on the cruise. Barbara, who had planned the cruise, was also one of the people on the cruise. It did not matter whether I was first at the table or last at the table, Barbara and I always ended up sitting next to each other. We had wonderful conversations as we enjoyed the delicious food. We had seen each other at singles meetings, but I thought she was unapproachable, and she told me later that she thought I was shallow. Actually, she is a quiet person, which can make her seem unapproachable. I am a person of many words so I have enough words for both of us. I am outgoing and exuberant, which can make me appear to be shallow to others.

There was something so very special about this cruise. I have been on cruises since then and it was nothing like these seven days. This was a God appointed time and set apart for His purposes. I was intrigued by Barbara and thought she was great, but I thought she was with another one of the guys on the cruise. So

I was content to be friends and just enjoy time with everyone in the group.

The first night on the cruise, we were sitting in a lounge area where people were dancing. One by one, the different members of our group got up to dance. I looked around and Barbara and I were sitting there just the two of us; so I asked her to dance. During that week, God kept putting Barbara in my path. I am a little slow, as many men are, and I didn't pay too much attention. After all, she was with someone else, so I thought.

On Tuesday for lunch I did not want to eat in the dining room. There are so many options on the ship. There was a little café serving hamburgers at the back of the ship, and I asked if anyone else was interested. The only one willing to go was Barbara. It was the best hamburger I had ever eaten, or maybe it was just the company. We so enjoyed just talking with each other. However, I was not looking for a relationship. I had my heart broken deeply more than once and could not bear another heartbreak.

Tuesday night at dinner was the only time we did not sit next to each other. It was fifties night and I dressed up like the *Fonz*. I had on blue jeans, a white tee shirt, and a black leather jacket, and don't forget the sunglasses. I really played the part. Cool and quiet, boy that was some acting! I sat across the table from Barbara. With the sunglasses on, I could look at her and she could not see my eyes. I sat there very stoic and did not say a word. She had previously thought to herself, isn't this guy ever quiet? But after that dinner, she said she liked the talkative Dennis better. Later, she mentioned that she could feel the vibes coming across the table and knew that I was looking at her. It made her feel uncomfortable and she was tempted to come rip the glasses off my face.

I found myself becoming more drawn to Barbara. She was kind and fun to spend time with. While in the port of Puerto Vallarta, she wanted to go see the Crystal Hotel. Her sister had told her the swimming pools there were amazing. I kept an eye on all the women in our group to protect them, as we were in a foreign country and I did not want any harm to come to anyone. I was not going to let Barbara go by herself, so I went with her. The pools were absolutely beautiful and beckoned to us. We were not in swimming clothes and had watches, wallets, etc. The water was so inviting that we came very close to just jumping in the pool clothes and all. Even to this day, we say that we should have jumped in.

On the way back to the ship, we began to talk about relationships and what I felt was the proper progression of a relationship. The first stage is friendship. Then, you become companions, where you spend much more time together. Finally, after marriage, you become lovers. While we were talking, she said later that she was thinking to herself, how long does this process take? Sometimes women, you must be patient with men. They are not known to move fast.

On Thursday evening, most of the group went dancing. Barbara and I sat down and began talking to each other. I asked her about her relationship with the other guy on the cruise. She said that there had been a desire for a relationship, but that no relationship existed. She then asked about my fiancé. What! A rumor had started that I was engaged to one of the women in singles ministry! After I got over my shock and expressed no knowledge of any such relationship, we realized that we were both unattached, and began to open up to each other. As we talked, Barbara said that God suddenly yet gently opened up her heart and dropped me in. When the evening was over, I walked her back to her cabin and she just knew that I wanted to kiss her (women's intuition). Instead, I took her by the hand and kissed her hand and said good night. She gave me this look of intrigue yet was pleased and honored. Chivalry is not dead. I firmly believe in treating women with honor and respect.

I had wanted to watch the sun rise over the ocean all week long and it was now Saturday morning, which was the last full day on the cruise. Each morning, a group would gather on the deck near sunrise to sing worship songs and pray. Each day I was too late to see the sun come up. As you get closer to the equator the sun rises earlier. Being the last day, I was determined to see the sunrise.

That morning there were a total of four people on the back of the ship, and with no explanation the other two left. Barbara and I were now alone on the deck. When I looked at the sky I was greatly disappointed. Since it had been raining for several days, the sky was completely covered in clouds. There was no way to see the sunrise. I had so wanted to be able to see the sunrise over the ocean. When all of a sudden, the clouds parted and the rays of sunshine shot through the clouds in a magnificent display of God's handiwork. The rays of light danced off the ocean. The gray and silver clouds now had a golden hue to them. God began to speak to me as the ship's engines churned up the water behind us. He told me that He was going to shine His light on my life and show me great and mighty things. What a special and unique God moment, and Barbara said she was honored to be able to share this God moment with me.

That afternoon, neither one of us wanted to stay in the cabins. After all, it was the last day of the cruise. Both of us, separate from each other, started walking around the ship hoping to run into each other. I wandered up and down each level of the ship but I could not find her. We kept missing each other as we walked around on different decks. It was a very big ship, and since neither one of us would just stand still it was difficult to find each other. It was so disappointing to not find her that afternoon. This was before cell phones so I could not just call her.

Finally, the evening came and we were going dancing for the last time on the cruise. We were in the Oklahoma lounge which was a very spacious and large room. The music was great and the evening was delightful, and as we danced we got caught up in the music. When we looked around we noticed that the lounge was completely empty. There was no one around, not even the ship's staff. It was just us and the band. The band graciously finished out their set for just the two of us. Barbara said that she felt like Cinderella at the ball dancing with her handsome prince.

As we returned to our cabins, we got on the elevator and our rooms were down a few levels. I got inspired and pushed the up button. She smiled with a big smile and I walked over to her and gave her a passionate kiss. I was not going to let that moment pass me by. Elevator rides will never be the same. This was the beginning of our lives together and we have been together since that day.

As a prologue to the cruise, after we arrived back to where most of the cars were parked, I needed a ride home. I agreed to let Barbara drive me home which was huge in our young relationship because I was still living in the neglected, run down, abandoned house. By now though, I had been able to make improvements so it was much better than when I moved into the house.

We stopped for lunch on the way home, and while we were eating, fear began to fill my heart. What if she dumps me? Will this be like previous relationships? What will she think about where I live? With all the rejections in my life fresh on my mind, I just couldn't get my heart broken again. I began to back pedal and considered ending the relationship before it went any further.

Barbara told me later that she asked God why I was backing off and He told her that I was just afraid. He also told her that she would have to earn my trust. She knew that consistency and loving me the way she has continued to love me through all these years would win me over. Growing in a relationship is definitely a process. Be careful to not rush past the time of friendship and getting to know about each other. If you do not address the obstacles and differences at this point in the relationship, it is only magnified after marriage.

Two days later, I had come to my senses and knew that I wanted Barbara in my life. Then to my surprise, I realized that I did not get her phone number or her address. Oh my, the first rule of meeting someone is getting that information. The Lord reminded me that all those months ago in the summer, she had made a flyer with that information. I searched frantically and found it in the back of my Bible. Barbara still teases me about not throwing anything away. I knew Tuesday was the best night in her busy schedule to ask her out. *The Titanic* was playing and just getting off the cruise, I thought it would be a great movie to see. Better to see it after the cruise than before.

I called her up and asked if she would like to have dinner and go to a movie. She said yes, so I said, "I will be right over." I immediately knocked on her door. I had called her from her front porch. The shocked look on her face was priceless. That was the beginning of a lifetime of surprises and spontaneity that we have shared together.

God says in Isaiah 55 that His thoughts are not our thoughts, nor His ways our ways. Only God could orchestrate such a wonderful plan to get me out of my world and mindset for seven days in order to get my attention and bring me the most wonderful person that has loved me unconditionally for all these years. God's plans for you are for your good, to bring you a future and a hope. Trust in God's timing and in His plan for your life. He will never let you down.

CHAPTER 10

Our Perfect Day

The cruise was over, but I now had a wonderful gift from God. My relationship with Barbara was now budding and so enjoyable each and every day. When God merged our hearts on the cruise, we both knew that there would not be anyone else. That's how amazing it is when God brings the one that is perfect for you.

When our relationship first started, our schedules were opposite each other. I worked nights and she worked days. I am grateful that she is a woman of prayer because after only 3 months together my schedule was changed to working during the day. That was miraculous and a story in and of itself. Because our schedules were opposite each other, at the beginning we spent a lot of time talking on the telephone.

One evening, as we were talking, we were sharing some things that we enjoyed and the things that meant a lot to us. I shared with her something that I had always wanted to do. It seemed like a lofty dream, but it was a hidden desire of mine all the same. I not only wanted to do each one, but do them all on the same day.

The day would look like this: Start out the day watching the sunrise from a lookout point in the mountains with the light beaming and the freshness of the morning. As the sun peaks over the mountain and begins to rise into the sky, it is such a special moment which brings the promise of a new day.

Secondly, go out to the desert and have a brunch to enjoy the desert air (not in the summer, of course). There is a certain fragrance in the clear, crisp air of the desert in the cooler months. Finally, end the day watching the sunset at the beach. Living in Southern California, the mountains, desert, and the beach are close enough that this was possible to do in one day.

As I was sharing the desire to experience all these in one day, Barbara said that sounds like the *perfect day*. Her statement just ignited inside of me, the perfect day. Wow. The only way that I could top off the perfect day was to ask Barbara to marry me. Right then and there I started to plan this special day. One of the things I really enjoy doing is researching potential purchases or the best products and so forth. I started immediately looking into where to go and how to make it work.

Going to the mountains was the easiest part of the plan as they are only about a 20 minute drive from where I lived. As far as brunch in the desert, the best time for brunch is on the weekend. Now trying to fig-ure out where to propose at the beach took more time and investigative effort. As I was developing the plan, knowing that we had met on a cruise, how appropriate it would be to ask her to marry me on a dinner cruise. The best option for a dinner cruise was in San Diego, which is about 120 miles from our area. Newport Beach was much closer but did not have any dinner cruises on the day I wanted to go.

I wanted to make this day very special and signifi-cant in Barbara's life, not just with the day itself, but I choose a special day in her life. Her anniversary with her late husband, who had gone on to be with Jesus, was on November first. I didn't want to take away from that day, but add to it by being a new beginning in both of our lives.

Looking at the distance between the three segments of our day, it was going to be about 440 miles round trip and that was going to be one long day. Even still, it was worth it, and I was going to try. The dinner cruise had the most details to plan. The right music, the right set-ting, and someone who could take a picture. I wanted everything to be absolutely perfect.

As a final step, I wrote out a letter. It began with, "Barbara my love, by the time you receive this letter, I will have already asked you to marry me." It included expressions of my heart, love, and the vision and hopes

I had of a great life we were going to share. After completing the letter, I planned to mail it the Saturday before our big day, as November first was on Sunday that year. This was a big step for me, because I had been rejected so many times in my life and had my heart broken deeply. What was even more amazing, I did not have a plan B or plan C. For those who know me, I always have a backup plan. There was only plan A, so everything was on the line. This time, I was so sure and my heart was at such peace. Yet, when I went to mail the letter, I hesitated knowing that this was the point of no return. No backing out now. I had such a confidence that everything would fall in place.

When I began planning, November was five months away. My plan was to propose to Barbara, but during those five months we never discussed marriage or our future together. Even though Barbara was very patient, she had her limits. In August she was getting concerned. Our relationship was now eight months old and no talk about our future. She finally got the courage to ask me one day, "Is this relationship going somewhere?" This is the one and only time in my life I gave a one word answer, as I am a man of many words. I said, "Yes." It was obviously God's grace in the whole situation, because she seemed content with that answer.

After all the planning and the details were in place, our perfect day was soon approaching. I had to work on that Friday, and as a truck driver each day was different. I never knew until that morning where my load was going take me.

I had designed and ordered an engagement ring in the shape of an infinity symbol, which was the last thing I had to do to be ready for Sunday. I had to pick up the ring on Friday afternoon before the 6:00 p.m. closing; so I could not be late.

That morning I was given a line load (which is over 100 miles from the terminal) with a backhaul (or another load) that I had to pick up in Port Hueneme in the Ventura area. The load took me to a delivery in Hemet and then to National City in the San Diego area. For those not familiar with Southern California, that is too far to legally drive for a truck driver in just one day. It also meant I would have to deal with the heavy Friday afternoon traffic in Southern California.

It was now late in the day and I was beginning to sweat bullets. I was getting nervous because it looked like I was going to get stuck in National City (near San Diego) for the entire weekend. I was almost out of available hours for the week. I was facing the possibility that not only would I not be able to pick up the ring, but the whole weekend could be a bust. After all the planning to make it perfect, it was crumbling and disintegrating right in front of my eyes. As I was making the delivery in Hemet, I was praying and asking the Lord to show me something. I need some peace and some direction to know what to do. My gaze went up toward the sky, still praying and asking God for wisdom. To my amazement, I saw a cloud in the sky in the shape of the infinity symbol, a perfect infinity symbol. I believe this was God's sign to me that everything was going to be okay. This calmed me down and then the thought came to me to call the dispatcher and let them know I was almost out of hours. If I made the delivery I would have to spend the weekend in San Diego. There was only one car to be delivered to National City, so the dispatcher told me to come on back to the yard. Praise God for His direction and His wisdom. He saved the weekend and I was able to pick up the ring just minutes before they closed. Whew, the weekend could now proceed as planned!

Sunday morning was finally here. I got up at 4:30 a.m. to drive the 20 miles to Barbara's house to pick her up. We drove up the mountain and found a large turn-out that overlooked the valley below. On a clear day you can see all the way to the ocean, however, this is rare. In the turnout was a stone pillar that must have had a plaque on it at one time. It was the perfect place to use for an altar. We had brought the elements with us and took communion together just as the sun began to rise. It was so fitting to start off our day with communion, breaking bread together and worshipping God. Putting God first is most important to us not only then but continuing until now and the rest of our lives. The sun seemed to rise slowly, especially at the beginning so we could take it all in. The brightness of the rays began to pierce through the fading darkness to the dawning of a new day. The sun was *shining brightly* which were the same words that God had spoken to me on the cruise where our relationship started. He was shining upon my life. We gave the first fruits of our day to the Lord and then we had hot chocolate and donuts. Everything was accentuated and seemed especially good.

We then drove down the mountain and out to the desert to Palm Springs, which was at least 70 miles away. You have to understand that the whole day had the hand of God on it. Barbara does not like to ride in the car very far or do road trips because travelling in the car makes her so drowsy and tired. That day she had such a spirit of adventure and was willing to happily go along with anything I suggested. She did not know what I had planned, and I unfolded the day to her one step at a time.

In Palms Springs, we went to a hotel that was serving brunch. It was very fancy and gourmet food. Barbara is not a big fan of gourmet food so the only thing she could find to eat was a waffle. We still laugh about her eating a 20 dollar waffle. I had planned and saved for this day so I was not concerned about the money.

My mind was fixed on the end of the day, which was to ask Barbara to marry me.

As we got in the car to return home, I suggested to Barbara, "How about going on a dinner cruise?" I made it sound like it was spur of the moment and spontaneous. She had no idea that I had been planning this for months. With the same adventurous spirit, she was willing to go.

Now on our way to San Diego, about 130 miles one way, obviously this was a God appointed day. We are just not this adventurous normally. We arrived in San Diego with several hours to spare before the dinner cruise would start boarding. One thing neither of us had ever done was go across the very tall bridge to Coronado Island. On the island is the famous Coronado Hotel which is beautiful and stately. We walked through the hotel taking in the beauty and the history of this famous hotel and then out to the beach next to the hotel.

I need to take a small detour here to give some background. Since our relationship started, I have sent flowers and written a poem of something fun or funny that happened that month to Barbara on the 30th of each month. I am what you would call a hopeless romantic. She is very practical and pragmatic, so she has had to get used to me showering her with these gifts. My main love language is gift giving, so ladies don't be too hard on your husband for not doing this. I tend to go over-board on my display of affection. Anyway, on October 30th as I was entering the flower shop to buy the flow-ers, the Holy Spirit told me to get red carnations. "It must be red carnations." He said it so firmly I knew that I better get a bouquet of red carnations.

Now back to the beach on Coronado Island. There had been some storm surf a few weeks before and the sand had been washed up into a big berm. We sat down on the edge of the berm and we were enjoying the late afternoon as we watched people walk by and seagulls fly overhead. After a while, the beach was quiet and we were alone with no one around. The tide was changing to high tide so the waves kept washing up closer and closer to our feet. A wave sent the water literally at our feet and when we looked down on the sand there was a perfectly shaped, freshly picked red carnation that had washed up by the wave at our feet. At first we thought that it had fallen off of someone like a boutonniere. We looked up and down the beach and no one was there. God had an angel drop a fresh red carnation in the wave so it could wash up at our feet. Barbara still has the car-nation pressed in her photo album of that day. What a confirmation that God had ordained us to be together.

That would have been enough of a miracle for us, but God was not done. As we sat there, we noticed the sky was overcast and cloudy. It was too cloudy to see the sun come down. We had wanted to see the sunset as part of our day, how disappointing to have it be so cloudy.

When all of a sudden, the clouds parted and formed what looked like an elevator shaft, just wide enough for the sun to lower over the ocean and set. We watched, yet amazed at the goodness of God to allow us to have our heart's desire. It was so astounding and we were in awe. God was smiling on this day. We had started the day off with communion and putting God first. God was putting His touches on this day as only He can do. Just as we both got to witness the sunrise on the back of the ship, we got to witness this miracle sunset at the beach. It was a God moment that had us floating on air as we got to the dinner cruise.

As we checked in to board the cruise, the staff confirmed to me that everything was set. It seems the whole staff knew what I was planning. Barbara still had no idea what was about to happen. On board ship, the dining room was so elegant, with candlelight and sparkling cider. The lights were glistening off the water in the bay and the setting was so enchanting. We have been on dinner cruises since then, but this night was enveloped in God's goodness.

I sat at the table across from Barbara so she would not notice the ring box in my pocket. The plan was, when we were finished eating, the waiter would come and take our plates. The DJ would then play the song

"Always and Forever." I was nervous so it seemed like an eternity before she finished eating. Finally, all was set. The music started, I asked Barbara to dance. When I turned her back toward the table, the DJ grabbed our camera (this was before cell phones, so it was an instamatic wind up camera). When the song was over, I reached in my pocket and took out the ring box. Pivoting on the ball of my foot, I spun around on one foot while I was dropping to one knee and flipped the ring open. Down on one knee I asked, "Will you marry me?" Barbara could not respond. She was still caught up in the smooth, flawless, and fluid motion in which I spun around. As she was gasping for her breath she said, "Are you kidding me?" She does not remember saying that as she said she was in shock. Yes, all those months of planning paid off. She was completely surprised. She was stunned not at the fact that I asked, but in the manner in which I asked. Obviously she said yes, because at the writing of this book we have been married over 22 wonderful years.

When the dinner cruise was over, I still had at least a two hour drive to drop Barbara at her house. About half way, I just could not drive any further as I was spent emotionally. Barbara took over driving while I slept. She was wide awake because she was still soaring. All those months of planning had really become a remarkable day. After I got home and had time to reflect on our day, I had to say it truly was—*our Perfect Day*.

CHAPTER 11

When the Unexpected Happens

By now, you know that my occupation was an automobile transport truck driver. My day consisted of loading and unloading cars and driving the freeways of Southern California in a very large truck. This in itself could be considered miraculous.

I had preloaded the truck with my delivery for the next day because the load was going to the other side of Los Angeles and I did not want to drive in the usual heavy morning traffic. By preloading I could get an early start. In order to make the load safe for transport, four chains are used to secure each car to the truck. If a chain should come loose it can be dangerous. Not only because of the potential of damaging one or more of the cars, but also because it's a fire hazard if the chain is dragging on the pavement causing sparks to fly.

As I was driving along the freeway toward my destination, I thought that I could hear the sound of a chain dragging on the pavement. I had already been driving for a couple hours so stopping for a break sounded like a good idea. This section of freeway was very hilly and in a more desolate area. I looked for a safe place to pull off on the side of the freeway to park. It was very important to get out and inspect the load to secure any loose chains.

I found a spot with a wide shoulder and was able to pull off well clear of traffic. The truck was 85 feet long when fully loaded so it was not easy to find a place to park it. Early in my driving career, I learned to put on gloves when dealing with a chain that had been dragging. The friction from the chain dragging on the pavement makes it very hot.

As I was exiting the truck, the first thing I did was reach for my gloves. I put my flip phone in my shirt pocket (early days of cell phones). There was a small field just beyond a hill where I had parked. It had a gap of about 10 to 15 feet between the back edge of the truck and the hill. As I was walking along the passenger side of the truck, I was looking at the load making sure that everything was secure and spaced properly. I put on my left glove, and as I was about to put on my right glove, I looked up and saw a Jeep Liberty coming straight at me, travelling faster than the other traffic. He was coming off the freeway at an angle that would bring him right between the end of my truck and the hillside. I was in the direct path of this vehicle coming and had no time to get out of the way. At first, I just paused trying to process what I was seeing. I would have no protection if the Jeep cleared the back of the hill. Everything was happening so quickly.

A vehicle traveling at 60 miles per hour travels at 88 feet per second. I was between 50 and 60 feet from the back of the trailer. I estimated that this driver was going at least 70 miles per hour, so I was less than one second away from being struck and killed. At the last split second, the Jeep made a sharp left turn into the back of my loaded truck. The only way I can describe what happened was it looked like the invisible hand of God just turned the front end of the Jeep towards the back of the truck. There were no skid marks so the driver did not apply his brakes and there was no evidence that he had turned suddenly. It appeared like he had fallen asleep while driving and did not wake up until he impacted my truck. As the Jeep veered suddenly into the back of the truck, it hit with such force that the cars on the bottom deck looked like an accordion that had been pressed together. The force was so great that it broke the chains that secured each car on the truck which was equivalent to 40,000 pounds of tension. Each chain will withstand 10,000 pounds of tension and there are four chains per car. There were a total of three cars on the truck that got severely damaged and sandwiched together.

The front end of the Jeep was driven up into its windshield shearing off the front right tire. As the tire came loose it rolled towards me with the axle and the brake line still attached to the wheel. While the tire was rolling at me, fragments of glass and metal from the car were flying by me. I was in a state of shock as I have never seen anything like this before. It was hard for me to react as I was almost frozen in place. This car was coming directly at me and should have hit me, but it suddenly changed direction and hit the back of the truck. As the tire was rolling towards me, I did not know how I was going to avoid getting hit. Fortunately, the brake line was still attached and as the tire ran over the brake line, it caused the tire to fall over right in front of me.

Coming to my senses somewhat, I knew I had my phone in my pocket, but I still had my right glove in my hand. I could not figure out what to do with the glove in my hand in order to get the phone out of my pocket. It is hard to think clearly in a time like this. I finally managed to get my gloves off and was able to retrieve my phone. I called 911 to get the emergency services on the scene. I really did not think the driver had survived. As I sat in my truck to get composed, I called the dispatcher of my company to report the incident. They calmly walked me through what to do. It was obvious that I was still shaken. Each truck was equipped with a camera for emergency situations or traffic accidents. I was instructed to take pictures and to use up the whole roll of film documenting the scene and the damage. The highway patrol had arrived first. By the time I got out of the truck, the ambulance was already there at the scene. In such a remote part of the freeway, I wondered how the emergency services had responded so quickly.

As I approached the Jeep that had hit the truck, the driver's door was open and I was afraid to look. I just knew he was dead. When I did look, there was no one in the vehicle. I asked the ambulance attendee where the driver was and he pointed to the side of the road. He was calmly sitting up on the side of the road and his only injury was a dislocated shoulder due to the seat belt shoulder harness. The fact that he had no cuts or bruises was miraculous. Not only had God protected me, but he protected this man from certain death. Our God is such a God of compassion and mercy. Once again, I was in awe of the hand of God protecting my life and being surrounded by His protection. *Is this the one who relies on the Lord? Then let the Lord save him! If the Lord loves him so much, let the Lord rescue him!* (Psalms 22:8, NLT).

As my co-workers and supervisors looked at the severity of the damage and condition of my load, they could not believe that the driver survived. I really believe that he is alive because of God's grace and favor upon my life and God's compassion for this man. God spared me from much sorrow that day. Had this man lost his life, it would have greatly impacted my life for years to come. It was a witness and a testimony to those I worked with of the mighty God we serve.

I heard a saying once that said, "Life is what happens when we are busy making other plans." Needless to say, my morning did not happen at all like I had planned. There was no way in the world I could have predicted a speeding car coming straight at me. To see the car miraculously moved by the hand of God into the back of my truck in order to save my life was extraordinary. When I have told others my story in detail, I would usually get the same reaction: WOW! If I then showed them the pictures, they would react even more emphatically with shock and surprise at the extreme force of the impact.

Soon after this incident, I realized none of this took God by surprise. In fact, nothing takes God by surprise. We are the ones astonished by God's actions, even if we were praying for them. There is a story in the book of Acts chapter twelve when Peter had been imprisoned and many were gathered in earnest prayer for him. After a series of miracles, Peter was supernaturally set free and found his way to where the prayer meeting was being held. When Peter knocked on the door, a young girl named Rhoda came to answer the door. She was so overjoyed when she saw Peter that instead of opening the door, she ran back inside and told everyone, "Peter is standing at the door!" Everyone thought she was out of her mind, but they eventually came and saw him for themselves. They were so *astonished*! They were the ones saying WOW! (only a guess on my part).

My miraculous experiences have helped me to recognize and catch a glimpse of the sovereignty and power of God. The prophet Jeremiah expressed it so well, *"Ah, Lord God! Behold, You have made the heavens and the earth by Your great power and outstretched arm. There is nothing too hard for You"* (Jeremiah 32:17, NKJV). Although my divine deliverance was such a small thing for God to do in comparison to the greatness of His creation, it was huge to me. Come to think of it, any miracle, no matter what the size or magnitude, is huge and exhibits the supernatural power of God!

So when the unexpected happens like this, it will cause these three things that just so happen to spell **W.O.W.** Miracles will cause us to:

WORSHIP

When the Lord supernaturally moves in our lives, it should bring us to a place of worship, not just for what He does but for who He is. The Lord had made a covenant with the descendants of Jacob and commanded them, *"Worship only the Lord, who brought you out of the land of Egypt with such mighty miracles and power. You must worship Him and bow before Him; offer sacrifices to Him alone"* (2 Kings 17:35-36, NLT).

My incredible life-saving episode brought me to such a deeper relationship with the Lord and an intense desire to worship Him. I found there is nothing greater than to come into the magnificent, sweet presence of Almighty God to worship Him from the very core of our being. For you see, worship is the total surrender of who you are, to love God for who He is, and to give Him all glory and honor for what He has done. Worship is an intimate expression of an elevated level of gratitude that reflects the worth of God. The wonderful works of God display His very character, nature, and attributes. Since we were created to worship Him, it is no wonder we get blessed when we do.

OBEY

One of the most remarkable examples of obedience is found in the book of Genesis. Years before, God had told Abraham to leave his country, relatives, and his father's house and go to a totally different land which God would show him. Abraham did not know where he was going but trusted God. When Abraham did what God told him to do, he was extremely blessed, became famous, and was given a promise that he would become the father of many nations.

In the 22nd chapter of Genesis, God commanded Abraham to sacrifice his only son, Isaac, as a burnt offering. Abraham had already experienced the miraculous birth of Isaac in his old age of 100 years old. He did not question God about offering up Isaac; Abraham's response was immediate. Romans 4:21 tells us Abraham was fully convinced that what God had promised He was also able to perform.

It is interesting that the word worship is used for the first time in the Bible in Genesis 22:5 to describe Abraham's obedience. As the story goes, the angel stopped Abraham from killing his son and miraculously provided a ram for the sacrifice. It was such an astounding miracle that Abraham called the name of the place, The-Lord-Will-Provide; as it is said to this day, *In the Mount of the Lord it shall be provided* (Genesis 22:14, NKJV). God then reiterated His promise: *In your seed all the nations of the earth shall be blessed, because you have obeyed My voice* (Genesis 22:18, NKJV).

There are countless benefits given for obeying the Word of God, and it is up to us to do our part. Realize that God will not ask of us anything that we are unable to do. When He asks us to do something, He will provide whatever we need to accomplish it. The expectation of obedience is God's part, but the bountiful blessings, the rich rewards, and the marvelous miracles (all the WOW factors) are ours *if we choose* to obey God's Word.

WONDER

This is the most obvious part of WOW because it is the easiest to express and relate to. It is fascinating to know that the word translated "wonder" in the original language of the Bible in some cases means a *miracle*, while other times it means *astonishment* or *amazed*. Either way it might come as an unexpected and pleasant surprise. We see both words being used in the healing of the lame beggar at the Beautiful Gate in the book of Acts chapter three. Verses nine and ten describe the reaction to the miracle: And all the people saw him walking and praising God: *And they knew that it was he which sat for alms at the Beautiful Gate of the temple; and they were filled with wonder and amazement at that which had happened unto him* (NKJV).

Experiencing a miracle or witnessing one in others can have the same effect of being filled with wonder and amazement. I am awed by the power of God working in my life as a mere mortal. God is a God of wonders and He never stops doing wonderful things. It never ceases to amaze me how in even the smallest of situations, the all-powerful and loving God puts His super on our natural. There is no small wonder that God wants us to live a life of WOW! He wants to do great and mighty things in our lives. As a result, these miracles should cause us to worship Him for who He is, obey Him from what He says, and be in wonder of Him for what He does. For

His marvelous works will testify of His greatness and power in our lives –

WHEN THE UNEXPECTED HAPPENS

CHAPTER 12

Freedom to Love

Freedom, this is a word that we used to not think about very often in America. Of course, we celebrate it every July, but you don't know how much you truly appreciate it until you don't have it. My wife, Barbara, and I discovered this on our first mission trip to the Ukraine.

They are not able to take pleasure in all the liberties that we take for granted here. They might not have the political freedoms that we enjoy, but the one thing they do have is big hearts! At all the churches, missions, home cell groups, prayer meetings, and fellowships our team ministered at, we encountered Christians with hearts absolutely on fire for the things of God. These precious people had a freedom to love in greater depths than I had ever known in my life. They passionately loved God with all their heart, soul, mind, and strength. They also demonstrated a great love for our team that was truly overwhelming.

I desired to have that kind of deep, passionate love igniting my heart so I too could have that freedom to love. The Lord granted my desire in a most unusual way. At the beginning of the week, my wife, myself, and one other team member as well as the young interpreter were sent to a city to minister at a crusade. We all crammed into this miniature car that somehow doubled as a taxi. We found out real quick that this was not going to be a luxury ride. Like most cars there, the windshield had numerous cracks and the air-conditioning was literally the windows rolled down. In addition, the shocks (if there were any) were almost useless driving through the cratered streets. You thought our potholes were big! Once we got onto a somewhat paved road, we could almost feel the road beneath us by the seat of our pants. To add to the adventure, the driver (who did not speak English) played a mean game of dodge car on both sides of the roadway.

About halfway into our journey we stopped for petrol. All of a sudden, we heard this unusual sound. *Clip clop, clip clop.* As we looked up, we saw a small horse drawn cart. It felt like a scene from *Fiddler on the Roof.* What a contrast, to be driving in an automobile and see a cart that would be used in the early 1900s. The people that live in the small villages use what they can to farm and earn a living for themselves.

Now back on the road, after two and a half hours we finally arrived at the mission center. There we were welcomed like famous celebrities and fed like royalty. By now, we were feeling pretty good about ourselves, these hotshot Americans ready to preach up a storm.

A van type bus then transported us another 30 minutes to the crusade location. The road kept getting more and more rustic until we found ourselves traveling up a dirt road. The bus came to a stop in a small village in front of a concrete block building. It was a very small building with just one door. As we walked inside, our hearts sank. We were expecting a crusade, yet our audience was a small handful of elderly people sitting solemnly and quietly with their heads bowed down. There was no appearance of life in the room. We thought to ourselves, "We flew halfway around the world and three hours of dangerous driving for this?"

What happened next changed our lives forever. The Lord spoke to us and told us that He left the 99 sheep to find the one that was lost (Luke 15:4-6). If you have loved the least of these, you have loved me (Matthew 25:40). Not only were we humbled, but also the Lord began to flood our hearts with His love and His compassion in such a measure that it was incomprehensible. We found ourselves loving the people just as Jesus would. We shared from our hearts as His love poured forth, filling the room with His presence. I found myself asking this question of the Lord, "How can I show you that I love you?" The Lord answered by saying, "Pray for each one of them." Just like when Jesus would lay hands on people, we witnessed God healing and the people getting set free.

Each one of us received a special touch of God's love that day. It was clearly evident by the healings that took place and by the sheer radiance on all of the faces. Where there once was no life, now everyone was singing and laughing.

We were not aware of the three hours to get back to the rest of the team as our hearts were in awe at the depth of God's love. *When you abide in the love of Jesus, your love is complete, mature and you walk and conduct yourself in the same way that He walked and conducted Himself* (1 John 2: 5-6, AMP). Now because of this experience, these verses in the first epistle of John suddenly came alive. I not only understood what John had written, but also now had experienced it.

How can we know this kind of love? How can we demonstrate this personal self-sacrifice for the betterment of others? How can we put on this love that can never fail? We must abide in His love. Abide (continue to live, stay, and dwell) in His love and you will truly walk as Jesus walked. Then, and only then, greater than you ever thought possible, will you experience -

FREEDOM TO LOVE

CHAPTER 13

Hand of God

Working as an auto transporter was a very unique job. One thing that was unique about the job, especially if you were ambitious, was that you could get paid for your effort. You could get paid by the hour or you could get paid by the load with incentive (a bonus program), whichever was greater. If the day was going well and if you were working under the incentive program, you could make more money in less time. It was always fun to challenge myself to work more efficiently and make more money at the same time.

There was a particular day that I was doing well and working at a good pace. The load took me to El Monte, California. This stop was on Valley Boulevard which was a very wide street with two lanes on each side and yellow stripes for the center median. I had to park the truck in the center median as there was no parking along the curb. The truck was facing east and the car dealership where the deliveries were made was on the driver's side of the truck. This was not a safe place to park, but there were no other options.

That day, I was making record time on the deliveries and was excited about the potential to make a good amount of money. Doing things faster, better, and more efficient is how I like to work. At this point, I was literally running to get each car delivered. The center median was only about eight feet wide and the hydraulic controls that move the ramps up and down were on the passenger side of the truck. After each car was delivered to the dealership lot, I ran back across the street to get another car.

As I learned the hard way from my childhood, you don't run between parked cars without looking. Being very cautious and looking both ways, if the traffic is clear, I was running as fast as I could. All the cars were now off of the bottom of the trailer and I needed to run along the opposite side of the trailer to use the hydraulic controls. These controls would slide the ramps to create a bridge to allow me to take the final cars off the upper deck of the trailer. Running at full speed, and I am not a small person, I had looked to my left to check the opposite flow of traffic. It was completely clear, so I jumped over the truck ramps that were leaning on the pavement. Looking to my right to make sure the oncoming flow of traffic was clear, I then proceeded. On Valley Boulevard you can see a long way, and there was no traffic coming all the way back to a signal which was red. It is very important to know where the traffic is coming from and how fast the cars are approaching to know how much or how little time you have to work the hydraulic controls. As the cars get close, there have been times that I have had to jump onto the trailer to avoid being hit by a car.

It was a beautiful day, there were no cars coming, and I was running full blast as I jumped over the ramps. Just as I was ready to turn left around the truck, I looked to my right to check for traffic. All of a sudden, what felt like a huge right hand hit me in the center of my chest. In a full run, at my size, I am not easy to stop. Yet this hand in my chest stopped me right there in my tracks. My feet left the ground from the force of the stop. It was a very sudden stop, but yet it did not hurt me as it was a soft yet forceful hand. I was so startled that I said out loud, "What was ..." I could not even finish what I was saying, when VROOOM a car driving on the wrong side of the street came racing by. Right next to the truck with four teenagers in the car, it went speeding by me. If the hand of God had not stopped me, I would have been a hood ornament on that car. I was just a split second away from a very serious injury if not death. Once again, I saw for myself how the hand of God is on our lives as believers for our protection.

In all the miracles that I had experienced up to this point in my life, this was the most significant physical intervention by a supernatural force. This incident had absolutely no logical explanation. Just the fact that I was stopped so suddenly in my tracks at a full run and with such an impact that my feet left the ground was utterly remarkable. The more amazing thing was that I was not injured in any way. Not a single bruise or an ounce of pain or discomfort. All of this taking place, preventing me from being hit by a speeding car, really made me grateful for the hand of God, literally, on my life.

This brush with death caused me to look into the Word of God to find out more about the hand of God, even more specifically the right hand of God. I cannot explain the impression I had that it was the *right hand* on my chest. By the position of the truck, the approach angle of the car, and the path of my run, it seemed like a good move to stop me. With a *straight arm* or perhaps a *body block,* to use football terms, is how God chose to save me.

The Bible describes the hand of God as a symbol of His power and strength. When it is upon a person it signifies God's favor and testifies of God's greatness. There are so many areas we can experience the hand of God. Here are just three of the ways that I have discovered.

The Hand of God Saves

We must realize that when His hand saves, it does not necessarily mean the absence of dangerous situations, but that God can keep us safe *through* them. God is with us to guard us and to protect us, even causing bad things to work for our good, for our deliverance, and especially for His glory.

In my case, He saved me from certain injury or death, showing His marvelous lovingkindness by His right hand because I trusted in Him (Psalms 17:7). If you want to see the many great and wonderful ways God has His hand on you, trust in, lean on, and rely on the Lord. Then pay close attention to even the smallest of ways that He moves in your life to protect you.

The Hand of God Secures

Just as any good shepherd protects his sheep, Jesus' protection is available to every believer who puts their trust in Him. The security of the sheep is not based on the sheep's ability to protect itself. Be assured that it is based on the awesome ability of the Good Shepherd to protect and preserve His flock.

How wonderful it is to know that absolutely no one can snatch His sheep out of His hand or the hand of the Father, *who is greater and mightier than all else* (John 10:27-29, AMPC). He secures us by His mighty power and His divine protection. *Fear not, for I am with you; be* not dismayed, for I am your God. I will strengthen you, Yes I will help you, I will uphold you with My righteous right hand (Isaiah 41:10, NKJV). The most secure place in the entire world is in the righteous right hand of God. Choose to follow Jesus closely, know Him intimately, and listen intently (John 10:3-5) to have His divine protection and reassurance of your security.

The Hand of God Satisfies

When God opens His hand, it is a display of the immeasurable and limitless greatness of God's power and strength. Know that God alone can truly satisfy (Ecclesiastes 3:11, AMPC).

His generous hand is superabundantly more than enough to satisfy every longing (Psalm 145:16, TPT), fulfill every desire, as well as protect those who love Him (Psalm 145:19-20, NLT).

I have come to greatly appreciate the confidence of living in complete satisfaction when I know God has my back—especially saving me from near death experiences. If you want to experience the hand of God on your life, then begin to hunger and thirst for righteousness and seek God first with a whole heart. I can tell you firsthand, that He truly satisfies the longing soul and fills the hungry soul with His goodness. *You will be satisfied with a full life and in all that God does for you. You will enjoy the fullness of His salvation!* (Psalm 91:16, TPT).

My sincere desire in sharing this testimony of God's intervention is to bring you to a place where you may trust, revere, and fear the Lord your God as you hunger and thirst for His righteousness. May you personally experience and know divine protection that saves, secures, and satisfies your life - all by the mighty hand of God!

CHAPTER 14

Career Ending But Not Over

The 1955 Chevrolet Belair V-8 2-door coupe—what a classic! It was the first car I had a memory of as a small child that my parents owned. There was a lot of room in the back seat to wrestle with my older brother (no seat belts back then). It seemed like just yesterday that I saw my dad pouring oil into the engine of that Chevy using a funnel. It made me so confused because I had just seen the *Wizard of Oz*, and I wondered why he was using the Tin Man's hat. Seeing my dilemma, my dad just smiled as he lovingly picked me up and gently sat me on the front fender of the car. He graciously explained the *other* use of the funnel by turning it upside down and directing the flow of the oil down into the small hole on top of the engine. He showed me how much easier it was to pour the oil into the wide part and made it fun to watch it disappear. Then, to my sheer delight, he let me pour the rest of a quart into the funnel. I got such a kick out of being able to *help* my dad.

It was this precious memory with my dad that helped me recently while I was experiencing an extremely challenging time in my life. This time, however, it wasn't oil that was on a downward flow—it was my life.

I severely injured my right wrist while on my job and was in excruciating pain. Two orthopedic surgeons agreed that surgery was the only possible option to salvage the usefulness of my wrist. Prior to the surgery date, I developed a serious blood clot in my leg. The surgery was quickly cancelled because it could now be life threatening, and it was too risky to operate. While battling the blood clot, with daily shots, and pills, and numerous weekly doctor visits, the pain in my wrist seemed to intensify. As weeks turned into months, my health continued to suffer. I was only able to sleep an hour or two at a time. Exercise was out of the question as it even hurt to take a walk. As a result, I gained 25 pounds due to inactivity. The lack of use of my right arm caused it to weakened and developed atrophy. To continue with the downward trend, the Workers' Compensation insurance company stopped paying benefits. With no money coming in, the inability to work or to have surgery to get back to work, the fight against mental anguish became extreme.

A few months into the second year of this ordeal, a bright spot emerged. A third orthopedic surgeon elected to perform the surgery. Although agreeing that surgery was necessary, unlike the other surgeons, he was confidently optimistic about a very favorable outcome. I was only a few years away from full retirement and wanted to get back to work. Unfortunately, Workers' Compensation denied the surgery and subsequently wanted to settle my case out of court. In order to receive a cash settlement, I would have to agree to no future medical benefits and sign a letter of resignation from my job to retire early. Talk about being between a rock and a hard place!

At any time during this tremendous trial, it could have been very easy to have a pity party or complain to everyone about the sad situation. It was apparent that crying or complaining would not change my circumstances. I chose to trust in, cling to, and rely on what God said in His Word instead. I searched the scriptures just to get me through each day. By pouring my time into His Word, the Lord directed me into a deeper walk of faith. My life literally felt like it was being funneled into faith. This brought back the precious memory of my early childhood. Only this time, I saw my life disappearing into faith. It was then I knew, somehow, some way, everything was going to be alright. It is from this life lesson that I would like to share with you three things about faith.

Faith Will be Tested

Trials are only to test our faith, as fire tests and purifies gold (1 Pet. 1:7, NLT), but they sure are not much fun. Yet, since our faith is far more precious to God than mere gold, trials will come. It is important to know that having our faith tested will be an opportunity for joy and will always be for our good and God's glory (James 1:2-4). Read those verses. It takes faith just to do verse two: *count it all joy when you fall into various trials.* The promise of this verse is you will be complete in your life, lacking nothing. God gets the glory when you let Him turn your tests into testimonies. (Testimonies always come after the tests). Except for my wife and a very few close friends, no one suspected that I was in such pain and anguish and facing potential financial disaster. When you're truly walking by faith, others won't know you are in a crisis.

Faith is a Matter of Trust

Faith is wholeheartedly trusting in Almighty God and every word He says in the Bible. *Every word* not just the ones we like or the easy to believe verses. His Word can always be trusted because it is impossible for Him to lie (Hebrews 6:18). Since it is impossible for God to lie, then God must always be telling the truth.

Truth is faith perceiving as real fact what is not re-vealed to the senses. (Hebrews 11:1c AMP). When sur-gery was no longer an option, I trusted God when He said, *"For I will restore health to you and heal you of your wounds"* (Jeremiah 30:17, NKJV). I spoke and declared this in confident faith, in spite of the times that tears were streaming down my face due to pain or I was crumbling to the ground in utter agony. I believed what He said, *"By His stripes you are healed"* (Isaiah 53:5, NKJV). His healing truth was manifested months later, and in an instant, the pain was gone. I was healed!

With no income and my savings almost completely gone, I trusted God when He said, *"And my God shall sup-ply all your need according to His riches in glory by Christ Jesus"* (Philippians 4:19, NKJV). One month after the settlement agreement with Workers Compensation, I received a cash settlement. I also received a disability check that was backdated to six months after my injury date equal to 18 months of benefits. Where I was once facing financial ruin, my accounts had now been abun-dantly replenished.

Faith Always Brings Triumph

Victory only comes when there has been a battle, conflict, or test. My work injury definitely conflicted with my life and tested my faith. However, we are told to overcome or triumph in the face of any opposition or challenges: physical or spiritual. How is this so? The Bible tells us a believer is a world conqueror by means of his faith. The secret of our continuing victory is obedience to the Word of God (1 John 5:1-5). Against all common logic, I accepted the settlement only in obedience to God. As it turned out, disability and the job resignation made me eligible for disability retirement. If that wasn't miraculous enough, on the day of my resignation, the company I worked for closed its doors. I would not have had a job to go back to even if I had the surgery. *Now thanks be to God who always leads us in triumph in Christ* (2 Corinthians 2:14, NKJV).

Faith and obedience are always partners in victory.

Although this period of time in my life was extremely challenging, it changed my life for the good. I am able to trust God when a test comes because I know it will refine and purify me. I can believe what God says because faith is a matter of trust. Because I learned how to trust and obey Him, God will direct my path to victory. Faith is not knowing what the future holds, but knowing who holds the future. Therefore, let your faith be tested, let God be trusted, let your faith be triumphant, as you let your life be - FUNNELED INTO FAITH.

CHAPTER 15

One Breath Away

There are always signs along the way if we know how to recognize them. For several weeks there had been small things like getting winded walking up a small hill and needing to catch my breath. Having no idea of what was about to happen and not recognizing the warnings, life went on as usual. Having recovered and healed from the wrist injury, I had no worries and life was good.

This is when it is especially important to meditate on the word of God daily and speak it over your life. It was a typical Sunday morning, and as I was getting ready to go to church, the Lord for some reason had me find and print scriptures on breath. This was the one that stood out: *The Spirit of God has made me, and the breath of the Almighty gives me life* (Job 33:4, NKJV). Rehearsing and memorizing this verse, I spoke it multiple times that morning. What an interesting verse I thought as I wondered who that verse was for that day. God will give me verses from the Bible to give to people to encourage them. It was later that I found out that this verse was not for someone else, but for me!

It was the first Sunday in April 2016. My wife and I drove to church as usual and parked the car. As we walked across the parking lot, approaching the rear entrance to the church, I suddenly found myself gasping for air. I could not breathe nor call out for help. The thought came to mind that this was not good. Realizing that I was on the verge of passing out, I went down on one knee and grabbed the bumper of a car. That was enough to enable me to take a small breath. In the midst of what should have been very frightening and unsettling, I was so calm and a tremendous peace enveloped me. Because I was so calm, my wife did not realize that I was in a crisis. We sat down for a moment to catch my breath and she asked if I needed to go to an urgent care center. When I said yes, she knew that this was serious. When a man is willing to go to the doctor, it must be serious.

At urgent care, after some tests, I was loaded into an ambulance and sent across the street to the hospital. I was diagnosed with acute massive bilateral pulmonary embolisms. In other words, massive blood clots covering both lungs. It was so severe that the doctors created a new category—acute massive. The doctor said that I was very lucky to be alive. Others called it a miracle. One doctor had never seen such a massive amount of blood clots on a person that was still living. My sister-in-law, a retired nurse, indicated that by the description of the CAT scan and all her years of experience, my condition is almost always fatal. If I survived, I would need the use of oxygen the rest of my life.

My God is greater! God's word is true and better still, *He who promised is faithful!* (Hebrews 10:23). Miraculously, the Word of God that I spoke over myself (Job 33:4) sustained me. Faith is a very present, urgently dynamic, power-packed, passionate expectation in God and a firm persuasion in His personal guarantee for the invisible. His word personally guarantees the impossible is possible. *He sent His word and healed you and delivered you from destruction* (Psalms 107:20, NKJV). The New Living Translations says snatched from the door of death. That is what happened to me; I was literally one breath away from eternity.

After five days in the hospital in the intensive care unit, I was released and sent home. Because this condition is usually fatal, I needed faith more than ever. As others prayed for me, it greatly stirred my faith to believe, I mean truly believe, and trust what God's Word says. I had to walk it out daily, as the recovery back to health was a process.

The first day my wife was to return to work and I was going to be home alone, there was an apprehension and concern. As I sat on the bed in the downstairs bedroom, because I could not climb stairs at this point, I wondered what the day would be like. Would I be okay? So many questions raced through my mind. As I looked up, I saw Jesus standing in the doorway of the bedroom. He spoke to me and said that everything was going to be alright. Wow, He truly is a very present help in time of need. That settled my heart and I began the process of healing.

When the process began, I could only walk 50 steps at any one time and was restricted to lifting under 15 pounds. It was necessary to use oxygen around the clock to maintain my life. Our God is amazing and true to His word. He truly watches over His word to perform it (Jeremiah 1:12). With this God kind of faith, I prayed, believed, and continued to take God at His word personally:

> *Who forgives all my iniquities, who heals all my diseases*
>
> (Psalms 103:3, NKJV)

> *He sent His word and healed me, and delivered me from my destructions*
>
> (Psalm 107:20, NKJV)

Who Himself bore our sins in His own body on the tree, the we, having died to sins, might live for righteousness—by whose stripes I AM HEALED
(1 Peter 2:24, NKJV)

As a result, I received an amazing revelation of faith. Most of the time sick people pray and believe God only when there is a manifestation of their healing. If you can see the healing, it is no longer faith. Manifestations of healing are not the *display* of faith, but the *result* of faith.

Now faith is the proof of things we do not see and the conviction of their reality [faith perceiving as real fact what is not revealed to the senses
(Hebrews 11:1, AMPC)

Here is the revelation: by faith *I KNOW* I am healed without any evidence that can be seen of this *TRUTH*. The fact of the diagnosis was evidenced by my need to use oxygen 24/7. It is easy to see that the *FACT* has to be overtaken by the *TRUTH*, because according to Hebrews 11:1, faith's evidence of the truth is not seen. Faith does not ask for any other evidence than the written Word of God.

This God kind of faith should be an integral part of every believer's life, not just healing. *NOW the just shall live by faith* (Hebrews 10:38, NKJV). This should really encourage you no matter what you are going through. God never gives us His Word without giving us the power and ability to accomplish it. As a born-again believer you can *now* live by faith. You have been given the measure of faith when you believed, and that's all the faith that you need. It is what you do with the measure of faith that makes the difference. Even small faith lived out in a big way absolutely makes a huge difference. Although your faith can be built up, increased, and strengthened, you have it *now*, so learn to use it. Your faith will stay dormant until a demand is placed on it.

After four months of diligently speaking the Word to my body and doing the work through exercise to build my body back up, I was released from the use of oxygen by the doctor. Praise God. Faith is the substance of things hoped for, the evidence of things not seen.

Use your faith now and believe the promises that will change your circumstance. If you want to see the invisible, to do the impossible, to move your mountains, and receive the promises, do it by trusting that God's Word will do what it says it will do. I am living proof that God's Word will not return void, but will accomplish what He pleases and prosper in the thing for which He sent it. Put your faith in God. It is the only way that leads to life.

CHAPTER 16

His Promise Fulfilled

In January of 2020, my father-in-law, who was 94 years old, decided he was ready to be with Jesus. He told me that he had prayed and talked to God about it and was at peace. He said that he was going to die and that he was ready to go home. This made me sad and troubled and when he saw my reaction he said, "Dennis, rejoice. I am going to be in Heaven. Dennis, rejoice. I am going to be with Jesus."

At that time, he had been living in assisted living with his bride of 73 years. My wife's parents have been such an example to me of godliness in so many ways. He was my research partner in putting together Bible studies for our marrieds' small group curriculum.

My own father had died when I was a teenager and so my wife's father had been in my life longer than my own father. He was a mentor and a spiritual example to me. He became dad to me. As he became weaker, we moved both of them into our house and arranged for hospice care. We would talk often, and one day he asked me to give him a Bible study about Heaven. Even though he was ready to go, he did not know what to expect and was apprehensive.

As I was looking through scripture and trying to figure out what to say to him, I asked the hospice nurse, who was a believer and appropriately named Faith, what it was like for her to experience people dying? She said it is different with each person. Some, it is easy, and others more difficult. Dad had been a person who dealt with fear most of his life. Even though he had a peace in his heart and he knew he was going to go to Heaven, he still had a fear about dying. It is like saying that everyone wants to go to Heaven but no one wants to die to get there. As he grew weaker, I did not know what to say. My attempts to comfort him did not seem to be what he needed.

During his life, he was such a kind and thoughtful person. And in his final days, he did something amazing. He began to call all the people he knew, from family to friends, to say good-bye and let them know that he was going to Heaven. Everyone was expressing their gratitude and thanking him for his love and example. They shared that they would not have been the pastor, or businessman, or parent that they were without his influence.

On Saturday morning, February 11, 2020, as we were eating breakfast, my father-in-law was sleeping nearby. We had an inspirational instrumental CD playing in the background. It is one of our favorite cd's with soothing and anointed piano and violin music that brings your heart into the presence of God.

All of a sudden, I was enveloped into a vision. I not only saw the vision but was also experiencing what I saw in the vision. It was like I became part of the vision. My wife and mother-in-law were sitting at the table with me but had no idea what was going on. It was like seeing into another dimension, yet becoming a part of what I saw. It seemed like I was in this vision a long time, yet my wife said it was only a few minutes.

In the vision, I found myself walking down a long hallway next to Dad toward heaven. At the end of the hallway was a wide opening. When I looked into the opening, all my senses were on high alert and extremely sensitized. As we were walking along, I looked over at Dad and to my surprise he was so young. He was now tall and straight. In his final days, he was in a wheelchair and was all slumped over due to age. He was nicely dressed and walked with his head held high. As we continued toward the opening, I was marveling at his appearance and his stature. All the concern about the process of dying now vanished and I was thinking about what was happening around me. I can now feel and sense the atmosphere. I can still hear the music that was playing in the background from the house but it was now behind us in the hallway. As we drew closer to the opening, the sounds of Heaven filled the hallway and everything else faded away. The music and the sounds of Heaven are without words. It was the most beautiful, incredible sound I had ever heard. It was like the grandest orchestra with many levels of instruments and sounds in perfect pitch and perfect harmony. The music encompassed the entire atmosphere of Heaven. It made the most beautiful and anointed music that we know on earth sound like a five year old playing chopsticks in comparison.

As we approached the opening, I was now standing slightly behind Dad, and I found myself unable to turn my head and look back up the hallway. I was so enraptured with all that was going on around me. At that point, the atmosphere of Heaven enveloped me. It surrounded me and I felt the most lavish love that is beyond anything I have ever known or imagined. An inexpressible joy filled my entire being along with a perfect, pure peace. The word pure is not pure enough to describe it. As I looked into the doorway, I could see a very brilliant light off in the distance. The light was brighter than the sun, yet it did not hurt my eyes. There was this wide, white street that came from the light towards the doorway where we were standing. It was like a road, and on both sides of the road there were thousands upon thousands of people lined up stretching into an infinity point, as far as my eyes could see into the midst of the light. The dimensions in Heaven are very different and my mind was trying to figure out how this was even possible.

I looked back at Dad and he had this huge grin. In life he didn't smile much, but now he was smiling with the biggest smile ever. As he stepped through the doorway, I looked up and the thousands of people lining the road were cheering, clapping, and praising God. They were rejoicing that he was finally there. When I looked again, there was another tier of people separate from those that were lining the road. They were distinctly different, yet there were two to three times more people on this second tier and the same thing all the way back to infinity. They also started cheering, clapping, and rejoicing that he was there. I asked the Lord, "Who are all these people?" He told me that these are all the people in Dad's lifetime that he has touched. He had been a pastor for more than 40 years, married for 73 years, and a Christian for 87 years. He was always helping and encouraging people. He truly had a pastor's heart.

While all this was going on, I was sitting at the table just crying. My wife did not disturb me because she realized I was having a God encounter. Still in the vision, I asked God who all these people were in the second tier.

I was told that they are the people who were touched by the people that Dad had touched. That is why there were so many, like the pebble in the pond ripple effect. Our lives touch more people than we will ever realize. The eruption of cheering and the celebration and rejoicing of Dad being in Heaven overpowered the sound of the music that filled Heaven.

As I was crying and overwhelmed, I did not know what to do. I just stood there. Dad never looked back as he stepped in and began walking up this white street. The white street caught my attention as I pondered what it was, and I could not understand it. It was not until two days later that I started researching, because I thought the streets were gold. I discovered that gold in its purest form is transparent. In Revelation 21:21 it states, *"And the street of the city was pure gold, like transparent glass"* (NKJV). The street appeared white like the brilliant light of God. The white I saw in the street was actually the light of God shining through the transparent street towards the opening where I was standing. The light was white and so much brighter than the brightest sunrise. It was so much brighter, brilliant, and refined as pure white, yet does not hurt you. God is love, and He is light, and His love will not hurt you. While standing there, it never occurred to me that I could enter in as well. I guess because it was not my time yet.

At this point, I gently *came to* at the breakfast table and began to realize I had returned. Earth seemed so inferior and almost disappointing. I was crying and it took time to compose myself. It felt like I was still glowing with the atmosphere of Heaven that had surrounded me. I could still sense the joy, peace, and love that make up the atmosphere of Heaven. It was so indescribable. I can still hear the music of Heaven in my heart. There were no words as I was still trying to take it in. It took me over a week of sharing this multiple times before I could stop crying each time I told someone, because it was so impactful in my life.

As I finished breakfast, I went over and immediately shared with Dad what I had seen. He looked up at me and said, "I believe that." He had been tense and still fighting to stay alive, even though he wanted to go. After this, he relaxed, and on Sunday morning, he peacefully left this life and stepped into eternity. Knowing this vision of Heaven made it much easier to rejoice for him. How could we sorrow when we know where he is and that we will see him again? The vision was so real. It was as if I was there. I experienced it. I heard, saw, and felt so surrounded by the atmosphere of Heaven and the music of Heaven. I was enveloped by the lavish love, perfect and pure peace, and the joy that was indescribable and full of glory. Words cannot describe this. My attempt to describe what I experienced is so lacking and does not begin to describe what I saw, felt, or heard. Even the grandest orchestra at Carnegie Hall does not compare to the grandeur of Heaven. Our hearts cry should be for the ability to impact lives like Dad did and to have a host waiting for us in Heaven because we walked on the Earth.

There was one more thing that God did. He showed me someone that I recognized in Heaven. He was a man who ran the local dairy in Colton, California where I was born and grew up. My father-in-law was pastoring the Colton Community Church and had lived in the Colton area for many years. My wife and I were both born in the same hospital in San Bernardino, California and spent our early years in Colton. At the age of 5, her family moved away, and at the age of 36, God brought her back to the area and eventually into my life.

Anyway, not to get sidetracked, this man that I recognized was a man that both of us knew from our past. This man was part of Dad's congregation and my brother's employer in his teen years. He was someone we had in common from our past. Even though I recognized him, he looked so different in Heaven. The word says that we shall all be changed. God's promise of Heaven will be fulfilled in all the lives of those who believe on Jesus Christ and whose names are written in the Lamb's Book of Life (Revelations 21:27).

I got the opportunity to get a glimpse of Heaven. The experience is undeniable in my life. It is as clear to me today as when it happened. Heaven is available for all those who are born again, who have received Jesus Christ into their lives. Unless you have accepted Jesus as your Lord and Savior, not just with your mind but with your heart, you will not see Heaven.

A man named Nicodemus in the Bible asked Jesus, "What must I do to inherit eternal life?" Jesus replied, "You must be born again." The Bible tells us, "But as many as received Him, to them He gave the right and authority to become children of God, to those who believe in His name" (John 1:12, NKJV). As a child of God, you are promised eternal life with Him. Why would you not want to be with God for all eternity in Heaven?

It is as simple as could be, for there are only two choices. Each person has to choose Heaven or Hell in this life. We cannot make the choice after we die. If you do not choose Heaven, then you are choosing Hell, even if you do not believe in Hell. There are no other options. Just as each person is destined to die once and after that comes judgement (Hebrews 9:27 NLT).

Make the choice today to receive Jesus into your heart. Not only will you get the benefits of Heaven, but also in this life you can have all that God has promised. In all the years I have lived and the things I have lived through, I know that God is real, that He loves me, and that He protects me. I have seen a glimpse of Heaven and know it is a real place. There is no way to talk me out of it, because I know that I know that I know.

Do you know? Do you really know? It is a simple question. If not, make that decision today.

If you confess with your mouth the Lord Jesus and believe in your heart that God has raised Him from the dead, you will be saved. For with the heart one believes unto righteousness, and with the mouth confession is made unto salvation (Romans 10:9-10, NKJV).

It is your choice to make. God wants to receive you as His child and give you entrance into Heaven to be with Him. He also wants to bless and protect you while you are here. I do not know why I have needed so much protection, but God knows, and I am so glad He does. Jesus promises that He will never, never, never leave you nor forsake you. That is an amazing promise. He promises to surround you with peace and strengthen you with His joy. His love is so pure and so complete. The greatest miracle of all is the transformation of a life when Jesus comes to dwell in your heart. What is holding you back from asking Jesus into your heart today? Just say this prayer out loud and ask Jesus into your heart right now.

Heavenly Father, I come to you today. I give you all of my heart and all of my life. Come into my heart, Lord Jesus. Be my Lord and my Savior. Forgive me of my sins, wash me with Your blood, cleanse me of my past, and give me a future with You, Lord. I believe that Jesus Christ is the Son of God, that He came, that He died, and that He was raised again to life just for me. Let it be known that from this day on, I commit to follow You, Jesus, for the rest of my days. I declare that I am born again. I am saved and headed for Heaven, denying my presence in Hell. Thank you, Lord Jesus, fill me now with Your Holy Spirit. In Jesus' name I pray, Amen!

Epilogue

Until that day when we enter Heaven and see Jesus face to face, our life story will continue to be written. My life experiences may be different from yours, but God has given each one of us a story. The word of our testimony is powerful and needs to be told, no matter how small and insignificant it seems to you. Share boldly what God has done in and through your life. It is yours to tell, and it does not matter if someone believes you or not, your testimony cannot be taken from you. It does not have to be labeled a miracle for God to get the glory for what He has done in your life.

Many may view the stories I have shared as a *coincidence* or *being lucky*. God does not use coincidence or luck, because He is the Most High God, and with Him nothing shall be impossible. I cannot make these stories up; they are sometimes hard for me to believe and I was there. Nevertheless, I try to use each situation as an opportunity to show the goodness and greatness of our God. When a door is opened to share the gospel as a result of a miracle, and it leads to a person's salvation, now that is truly a miracle of miracles!

All that I am and all that I have has been shaped by the miracles I have experienced. May I never lose my sense of wonder at the miraculous working of God's mighty power. Miracles have transformed me by the boundless brilliance of His nature, changing my spirit to be more like Him. May you too be compelled to draw closer to the God of exhaustless love and build your faith through His infinite Word. I pray these stories have encouraged you to be strong in the sovereign and limitless power of the Lord and will strengthen your walk with Him.

God shows no partiality and is no respecter of persons (Acts 10:34, AMPC). It makes no difference who you are or where you are from. God is always working in the lives of those who love Him. He will show Himself strong on your behalf and even perform miracles when needed. You will then have your own story to tell and testimony to share. God truly wants to take you from faith to faith, from strength to strength, from glory to glory, and *FROM MIRACLE TO MIRACLE!*